To Kate

Wishing you happiness

Sport + life.

Ian . C.B. Taylor

Olympic Gold
Medalist.
8 . 5 . 89.

BEHIND THE MASK

BEHIND THE MASK

THE AUTOBIOGRAPHY OF
IAN TAYLOR

Macdonald
Queen Anne Press

A *Queen Anne Press* BOOK

© Ian Taylor with Cathy Harris 1989

First published in Great Britain in 1989 by
Queen Anne Press, a division of
Macdonald & Co (Publishers) Ltd
66–73 Shoe Lane
London EC4P 4AB

A member of Maxwell Pergamon Publishing Corporation plc

Jacket photographs – Front: Allsport/Dave Cannon
                       Inset: John Twinning
                       Back: Colorsport

British Library Cataloguing in Publication data
Taylor, Ian, *1954*
  Behind the mask,
  1. Mens hockey. Taylor, Ian, *1954–*
  I. Title
  796.35'5'0924

  ISBN 0–356–14520–4

Typeset by Selectmove, London
Printed and bound in Great Britain by
Hazell, Watson & Viney Limited, Aylesbury, Bucks

To Julie, Simon and Oliver.

For a person to win a gold medal it takes years of dedication, commitment and hardship, not only by the individual but more particularly by their parents, family and friends. This book not only outlines my particular road to success but is a tribute to the dedication many people have given in my quest for gold. To all these people, but especially Julie my wife, a very sincere thank you.

CONTENTS

1
SEOUL : THE FINAL CURTAIN

The impact of winning an Olympic gold medal didn't really hit me until the whole team stood on the rostrum in the Songnam Stadium. It was then that I realised that my lifelong ambition had been achieved. The pride of representing Great Britain, special thoughts of my family and a sadness that it was the end of the road were just some of the emotions that flowed through my mind as I stood there, watched by millions around the world.

It was an unexpected privilege to lead the team out to the medal ceremony because I had anticipated that the captain would have that honour. But this was done in numerical order and so, being number one, I walked out first. It was a real bonus because I had already carried the Union Jack at the opening ceremony at the head of the whole British Olympic contingent, and I felt another huge swell of pride when I led the hockey team out.

As I stood on the rostrum once we had been awarded the medals, I started to put into perspective what it all meant. I thought about how many British athletes had managed to win gold medals, I thought of the countries like Germany and Holland on either side of us that we had beaten to the final honour, and I looked towards the dejected Australians sitting in the crowd.

The climax of the occasion must have been the moment we turned round to face the flag and hear the national anthem being played. There have been many cases of 'so near and yet so far', but this time it was for real! When the national anthem started to play we all came back to being a team, united in the pride of being British. I'm normally completely tone-deaf and am probably one of the worst singers in the world, but at that moment joining in with the others as they sang was the most natural possible way of expressing my emotions.

My life has always had a very strong purpose and objective, in fact my whole lifestyle has been programmed towards attaining the gold medal. All of a sudden, I wondered how this would all change now that ultimate goal had materialised, and I couldn't help reflecting on how our fortunes had ebbed and flowed during the past fortnight.

Our first match of the tournament was on a hot Sunday afternoon against the South Koreans. Inexplicably, it was scheduled to take place on the second pitch which was not only much smaller in terms of capacity, but the surface wasn't the same as that of the main stadium. It was a different style of artificial pitch, a little bumpier than the main pitch and with several wet patches where the players often struggled to keep their footing. The spectators were very close to the field of play and there appeared to be an enormous amount of support for the home team. They had hundreds of cheerleaders and there seemed to be a Korean lending support from every possible viewpoint in the ground.

We knew it was going to be a very difficult game and I certainly considered the South Koreans one of the most underestimated teams in the tournament. They had already shown their potential prior to the Olympics by winning the Asian Games, beating Pakistan and India *en route*, and they had also recently beaten Australia and the Soviets. We realised that playing the home team in front of their home crowd and in hot conditions was going to be a testing encounter.

After weathering some early pressure we started to impose ourselves and took the lead in the first half, when Sean Kerly celebrated his hundredth outdoor international appearance with a brilliant fiftieth goal for Britain. Just after half time we went further ahead when Paul Barber scored at a penalty corner. But then we suffered a fateful loss of concentration and the Koreans came back at us to level the scores. Our problems were compounded by our forwards who were moving so quickly all the time that they constantly lost the ball, with the result that our midfield players became totally ineffective because they were just chasing up and down the pitch. This lead to all sorts of opportunities for the Koreans and they had a couple of chances to take the lead, but thankfully they didn't. In the closing stages our superior fitness and experience paid off, but despite the pressure we weren't able to redeem the situation.

We were very disappointed; although we hadn't expected to win by an enormous margin we had hoped for more than one point. It was the frustration of the first game. We hadn't really played well as a team, and our defence had shown some uncharacteristic weaknesses – the midfield had been ineffective and the forwards had gone off at great speed but achieved little. At that stage we knew that seven points would probably, although not definitely, be enough to secure us a place in the semi-finals but that eight would be a much safer cushion. At the outset we were anticipating losing two of those points and therefore the loss of one point to an unfancied team was a bit of blow.

Our game against the seventh-seeded Canadians was at nine o'clock in the morning and this time was in the magnificent Songnam Stadium itself. The weather was always much cooler at that time which suited us much better, and we cruised to an easy 3–0 victory. Left-wing Imran Sherwani put us ahead within three minutes, and second-half goals by Paul Barber and our captain Richard Dodds put us back on course. It still wasn't as convincing as it might have been, and we didn't put away all the chances we had. Apart from that aspect it was an uneventful game and I can hardly recall being called into action.

The next match was a crunch game against the reigning Olympic silver medallists, West Germany. A good result would make the difference between first or second in the pool and could also have taken off the pressure for the rest of the group matches. In our hearts we were confident in our ability but not in the way we had been playing. The West Germans were our old adversaries, and each and every one of us badly wanted to beat them.

They attacked us from the start but against the run of play, Paul Barber smashed in a penalty corner to give us an early lead. However, the Germans came back at us relentlessly and then, after successfully defending 11 short corners, their sweeper Carsten Fischer flicked powerfully into the net to equalise. I was very annoyed with myself because I felt that I had missed it rather than Fischer having scored it. A goalkeeper, particular one of my experience, knows when he should save a shot and I had that one in my sights and missed it. It was even more frustrating because we had clung to our lead for nearly an hour and my mistake had let them in. I couldn't possibly have dreamt of the drama that was about to unfurl with less than two minutes of the match remaining.

At yet another corner the Germans lined up with a double strike option – Andreas Keller coming in as well as Fischer. That meant I had to cover more floor space than normal and I had to get down quickly. Fischer was always liable to try another flick, so to be extra cautious I asked Paul to stand behind me on the line to eleviate any danger, just in case I couldn't get my hand to the shot. It was no surprise when the flick came in, and having gone down I was up on my feet instantly and couldn't believe it when I turned to see the ball go straight at Paul who fended it away with his stick. The Australian umpire Don Prior ruled a deliberate foul, and had no hesitation in awarding a penalty stroke.

It was a shattering blow, and I was completely numbed and angered by his decision. There is absolutely no doubt in my mind that the ball was going over the bar and was still on an upward trajectory when it passed my hand. It was to become one of the controversial issues at the Games, but in the end one has to learn to accept that the umpire's decision is final and that there is no point in protesting. What aggrieved us, however, was that although we weren't the best team on the day, we had worked for 68 minutes to earn a draw and now all our efforts were being taken away. The difference between the top teams in the world may often be that one save, that one goal or that one decision. Now I had to face the legendary Stefan Bloecher at the penalty stroke.

As I prepared to defend the penalty, I knew that I had an excellent chance of stopping the ball because Stefan normally goes high right and I have saved the last four he has fired at me. But this time I was caught in two minds. I had recently seen some videos of him where he feigned to go high right but actually converted them by going low left. By the time the umpires had ascertained that we were both ready, I was still unsure, and made the hasty decision to go low left even though he had lined himself up to do the opposite. I was wrong and Stefan gleefully made his way back to his jubilant team-mates to celebrate their last-gasp win. It transpired that he was so anxious about the fact that I had thwarted his last four efforts, that his only concern was to put the ball in the top right corner as hard as he could, and that misleading me was the last thing on his mind! He felt that if the shot was good enough I would have no chance.

The whole team felt terribly dejected after the game, and it was a forlorn side that returned to the athletes' village. I had previously thought that I had won my battle against Fischer, the hardest hitter of a ball in the world. But instead, my Olympic dream was beginning to crumble.

Our self-confidence was severely eroded and we were beginning to have serious self doubts. But looking back, those poor results probably did more for us as the tournament progressed than if we had gone through and held on to those three lost points. Those results, and their possible influence, made us that much more determined to go out and succeed. We were forced to sit down and evaluate our performances clinically and constructively.

Various pockets of senior players got together and tried to analyse the reasons for our poor showing. I would have long discussions with Richard Dodds, Sean Kerly and sometimes Richard Leman; another group would include Paul Barber, Jon Potter and David Faulkner. It was at the next team meeting that we set out our objectives, and by the end we all knew exactly what was required from every player. One thing was very clear: we had to win our last two games against the Soviet Union and India if we were to have any chance of qualifying for the semi-finals. It was the finality of the situation in which we now found ourselves that inspired us.

It wasn't until the second half of what had become a tough physical battle with the Soviets, on a warm Saturday afternoon, that we managed to break the deadlock. Inevitably it was Sean Kerly, who had regained his scoring touch, who did it when he pounced on a loose ball and slammed his shot past the goalkeeper. He flicked in another at a corner and Paul Barber made it 3–0 with a corner strike. A lack of concentration in the dying minutes allowed the Russians to rally and they sneaked one in with minutes remaining. That was a harsh lesson for us because if it hadn't been for that temporary lapse we could have gone into the India game needing only to draw to qualify. As it turned out, the goal difference was such that India had a better average than us, since they had crushed Canada 5–1.

The Indians, once the unchallenged masters of the game and eight times Olympic Champions, failed to provide us with any real opposition – I'm relieved to say – and we swept triumphantly past them to win 3–0. Paul scored his fifth goal of the Games, and once Sean had put us further ahead Jon Potter converted a stroke to secure our place in the semi-final. I wasn't surprised at how we destroyed the Indians with the chip ball up to our forwards. We never allowed them to get their short passing game going, and I was fully prepared for everything that they tried at the short corners. The lessons of the previous match kept us going, and we held on tenaciously to keep a clean sheet.

I think most people expected us to celebrate wildly afterwards, but that wasn't the case. We had gone to Seoul to win the gold, and naturally we had to get into the semis if we were to achieve this. Likewise some folk were beginning to worry that we might have been better off playing Holland instead of the top seeds, Australia, who had stormed into the semi-final from their pool. At that stage, however, it doesn't really matter – if you want to win the gold medal, you have to beat everyone.

We concentrated all our preparations, then, on beating the Australians – although, to be honest, it was no different to any of our other games. The management seemed to suffer more from nerves than we did, and worked themselves into quite a panic about all the different options the Aussies had at corners! I was quietly confident, though, that the Australians would be worrying about how to get past me because I felt I had had the better of our exchanges in recent games. Where I did feel we were vulnerable was in the open play situation. I thought that their free-running forwards would be far more likely to get into a one-on-one situation and create problems that way. The British team was now full of confidence and we were all familiar with the Aussies' style of play. In fact, I think that this was my twenty-sixth international against Australia. We also had the psychological advantage of having beaten them in Los Angeles, when we took the Olympic bronze.

We held them tightly from the start and patiently waited for the opportune moment. Once again it was Sean Kerly who opened the scoring at a corner, and he notched a brilliant second after being set up by Steve Batchelor. But within a minute the quicksilver centre-forward Mark Hager had pulled one back for Australia. And shortly afterwards Neil Hawgood equalised from exactly the type of situation that I had feared before we started: a mix-up in our defence allowed Hager to slip the ball to Hawgood who was unmarked. Suddenly a two-goal lead had gone and we were looking vulnerable. But with less than two minutes remaining and extra time looming, Sean featured in a superb move with Jon Potter and Kulbir Bhaura and completed his hat-trick to kill off Australia. The World Champions' dreams were in tatters, and we had reached the Olympic final for the first time since 1948.

I went up to the Australian Richard Charlesworth afterwards and held out my hand, but he refused to shake it. Apart from being one of Australia's greatest ever players, 'Charlie' is also a doctor and federal MP and highly respected throughout the world. Many years ago, when my international career was just beginning, I played against him in Australia and kept him at bay successfully. After the game he swore that one day he would put a hatful past me. I went up to him a second time to offer my hand, whilst gently reminding him that we would never play each other again and that he still hadn't got the hatful! Once more he refused. It was the end of his Olympic dream and he must have felt bitterly disappointed. It may have been 'unsporting' of him not to shake my hand, but I don't honestly know what I would have done in his place.

There were amazing scenes when the final hooter went, and I can remember everyone on the bench leaping up and rushing onto the pitch. Everywhere there were players hugging one another and Martyn Grimley was already singing 'we are the champions!'. The press and supporters poured onto the field, and many of us had to give radio and television interviews.

One scene that had drawn much attention amongst spectators was when Steve Batchelor was substituted. He was quite unable to watch proceedings for the last twenty minutes and, according to those who could see, he went and sat down behind the bench with his back to the pitch, and faced the crowd with his legs crossed just willing the team on. What made it even funnier was that he was wearing a silly red cap – a lucky one he insisted – and only when he knew we were in the final did he abandon the pose! He was absolutely thrilled to be interviewed by television after the game, particularly as he had been complaining good-naturedly that Sean had been getting all the attention. He was so excited, however, that we couldn't understand a thing he said!

I was able to keep quite calm throughout all the euphoria because as far as I was concerned I still hadn't achieved what I set out to do. At this stage I was still on target but I knew from previous experience that the big game was still to come. Too often we had failed the final hurdle, and I wasn't prepared to let that happen again.

There was a certain amount of celebration, and that night the BBC took us out to dinner at one of the best hotels in Seoul. The Sports Minister Colin Moynihan, who had been one of our staunchest supporters, also joined us. We were fairly restrained however – most of the lads drank orange juice and by ten o'clock we were all on the bus home!

For the first time in the tournament we now had two days' rest until we played in the final, which was scheduled for three-fifteen on Saturday, the penultimate day of the Games. The problem arose of how best to cope with the time in a harmless fashion. Some of the team went off to the Olympic village or went sightseeing, but within half an hour they were back with itchy feet!

We didn't get up particularly early on the morning of the final and we all went to breakfast in our own time. On match days I always have a very good breakfast because I find it difficult to eat properly before a big game. There was a huge amount of support forthcoming at breakfast from the other British athletes – most of whom had already finished their events – and several of them came up to wish us good luck. Our team meeting was at eleven o'clock that morning, but nothing terribly different to all the other games was said. The team manager Roger Self would always involve most people at some stage and then bring in our coach, David Whitaker. We had had a video session the day before and all the specifics had been discussed, which David now reinforced.

It was agreed that we wouldn't change our basic style but that our best method of beating the Germans would be to play the ball out wide and keep them at full stretch. It was also planned to chip the ball around Fischer at the back and keep him constantly on the move. We knew that we should concede as few penalty corners as possible, but nevertheless I was confident about defending them. Up front it was imperative that the forwards shouldn't lose possession. If they couldn't see their way through then they were to play a soccer-style pass back to the midfield coming up in support.

We knew that the Germans would be forced to play without their key midfield player, Stefan Bloecher, who had suffered a nasty head injury in the semi-final when the Dutchman Jan Bovelander had hit him at a penalty corner. Although a marvellously entertaining player, I believe that Bloecher has lost a great deal of his effectiveness in the last three years. Stefan is no longer as incisive as he was when he scythed his way through, and he doesn't score nearly the same amount of goals now. He will always bemuse and dazzle with his stickwork but all too often it's in front of a defence, and good defenders have proved this regularly. On an occasion like this, a forward like Michael Hilgers is far more dangerous, because he's an unknown quantity. He is extremely talented and is undoubtedly a world class player, with the appetite to become the next Bloecher. We hadn't had the experience against him and we didn't know what his strengths and weaknesses were. I'd seen him diving for deflections in some matches, which is a nightmare situation because then you not only have to save shots but you also have to cover for deflected angles.

I couldn't help noticing the different reactions of everyone at the team talk. Whilst the players were reasonably serious and quite obviously deep in thought about the game, it was the management's attitude that struck me. Roger Self had been pretty wound up throughout the tournament, and had at times been almost neurotic. Some of the senior players found it necessary to exercise a large amount of self-control themselves! But Roger had managed our problems very well concerning things like press interviews, special foods and so on. David Whitaker tried desperately to promote an atmosphere of calm, even though within himself he was obviously anything but! He tried to convince us that we had the ability to come out on top, and that if we showed control and poise then we could do it.

It was a lovely warm afternoon when we arrived at the stadium, and I sensed that there was an air of cool assurance amongst us all as we got off the bus and passed through security. Everyone seemed to know exactly what they were going to do. Various people shouted greetings to us and we responded accordingly. Australia were playing Holland for the bronze medal, and we paused for a while to watch. That was good for us, giving us a bit of mental relief, stopping us from getting too wound-up. We then ambled across to the dressing room, started getting changed and began our our stretching routine which usually lasted about half an hour. Our physiotherapist Kevin Walters – a former Wolves physio – was excellent as usual, not only on the physical side but on the psychological aspects as well. He was thorough and professional, and good for team morale.

The final preparations were in the changing room, where the shin pads were put into place and the last-minute taping of sticks was completed. Roger Self spoke to us, emphasising that the Germans were only human and concentrating very much on team motivation. Paul and I were then asked to speak from a personal point of view as to what winning meant to us, and in our own ways we tried to get the players positively psyched-up. The only way we were going to win was if everyone wanted to do so badly enough. We were going to have to die for one another out there!

We went through a final warm-up on the pitch, and as the tension reached its peak Richard Dodds had the last word. He said that all along we had stated that we were going to do it for our country, our friends, our family and so on, but that if we needed another reason, then what about doing it for ourselves!

The final began, and I remember West Germany getting a couple of corners early on. I thought they might flick them, but one was hit by Fischer and the other one by Keller, who was appearing in the final on his twenty-third birthday. I had to get down very late to them, since I had delayed until the last possible moment in an attempt to put them in two minds – whether to flick or to hit. I stopped the shots on the underside of my arm, and although they really hurt I was pleased because I had won this initial skirmish with the opposition.

Imran Sherwani gave us a first-half lead, when he skilfully worked the ball into the net following good build-up from Sean and Steve. At half time Roger stressed that we must keep the game tight, and remember the basics. He said that as long as we could keep up the discipline we had shown so far, he saw no reason why the result should change. Whatever happened, it wasn't to develop in to a ping-pong type situation where they would bombard our goal and we would do the same to them. The players' message to one another was to agree that it was going well, but towards the end of the first half it was felt that the forwards were tending to run away again and that they should slow it down a bit and choose which times they were going to break through. Another of the tactics we decided on was to use the chip ball more often to try and get our opponents' midfield players running up and down. This would make them far less effective, and eliminate the short passing game that the Germans not only enjoyed but were very good at. Martyn Grimley would play a lot tighter in the second half and keep the reins on Thomas Reck, the dangerous right-wing.

About ten minutes after the break, Sean put us further ahead when he scored at a penalty corner. Paul had slipped the ball to him after the German defenders had fully expected him to have a go at goal. There wasn't much time for Sean and I'm convinced that he totally mis-hit the shot, because it barely hit the backboard, but it was all that was needed to deceive the German goalkeeper.

Imran delivered the killer blow when he scored the third, after Steve had done brilliantly to receive a chip pass from the back, eluded two defenders and centred a perfect ball. I think the Germans were at death's door at that stage, and I felt confident that they didn't have it in them to fight back. They scored a consolation goal towards the end, when their captain

Heiner Dopp did well to pick up a cross from the right and reverse scooped the ball past a diving Richard Leman. With under a minute left to play, one of the most extraordinary substitutions took place – and it concerned me! Apparently a new ruling by the International Hockey Federation (FIH) had stated that a player who had not taken part in a match at all would not be eligible to receive a medal if his team won one. Two of our squad, goalkeeper Veryan Pappin and defender Sam Martin, had not yet played and so, with the gold medal in our sights, the management made the hasty decision to send them on. Neither of them were aware of the situation, which was probably just as well, but it did mean that I was substituted for the first time ever in my career. Richard Leman came off to give Sam his opportunity, and I was happy to step down to give Veryan his chance.

When the final hooter sounded my first thought was 'I've done it!'. All the leaping up from the bench and the spontaneous hugging and congratulations came about 20 seconds later. I immediately wanted to go and thank all my team-mates, in the realisation that we'd all finally achieved it together. At the same time, I felt empty because my wife Julie and our two sons Simon and Oliver weren't there to share the special moment with me.

There was complete pandemonium within minutes. Relatives, friends, press and honoured guests were all clamouring to speak to us and we were surrounded by well-wishers. The Princess Royal, who had watched a few of our matches, came down to speak to us and meet the players. We considered that HRH was our lucky mascot, because from Los Angeles onwards, we'd never lost a single game she'd watched us play. Some players were crying, and others couldn't stop leaping about and indulging in back-slapping and jumping on each other's shoulders.

After all the initial celebrations, I went and sat down on the bench in the late afternoon sun and soaked up the glory. My first thought was of my eldest son Simon. Before I'd left, Julie and I had tried to explain to him that I would be away for a long time. As it's difficult to explain that to a three-year-old, we had gradually worked it so that Daddy was 'going away for a long time to the Olympics to win Simon a gold medal'. And we kept saying that to him. As I continued to sit there I thought: 'Simon, I really can bring home the gold medal for you.'

Julie and I did a TV link-up not long after that. She was in the London studios and I was in the Songnam Stadium, but whilst I was thrilled to be able to talk to her it was frustrating not being able to see her or give her a big hug.

I can remember all sorts of different people coming up to say congratulations. Trevor Clarke, the former Director of Coaching in England and now the Canada men's team coach, who was so influential in the early part of my career, came up and I thanked him for all he'd done. A Dutch reporter who had covered his first international the day I made my debut also offered me his best wishes. The Indian team were particularly enthusiastic about our victory, as were many of the Kenyans. After the medal ceremony I commiserated briefly with some of the Germans on my way back to the changing rooms – friends like Stefan Bloecher, Ekkhard Schmidt-Opper and Heiner Dopp, the wine farmer who sends me bottles of his vintages. When I got inside the dressing room I threw my pads up in to the air and let out a massive shriek. It was something most out of character for me because I'm normally pretty impassive and quiet. But the occasion had finally got to me, and I was at last getting rid of all the tension that had built up.

It's hard to explain my feelings once we had won the gold. I can only really describe them as a battle of directly conflicting emotions: the sheer happiness and the total emptiness, the excitement and the feeling of dejection, the yearning to share the joy with loved ones and them not being there to share it. But by the time I got to the medal presentation, all the positive feelings had returned.

Following the post-match press conference we went back to the village and then went out a celebratory dinner at one of the plush hotels in Seoul. All the Hockey Association officials, supporters and families were there and it was an excellent evening. Because we had hardly drunk anything alcoholic for such a long time it only took a couple of glasses of wine for most of us to feel quite merry! Richard Dodds gave a very humourous speech, with some irreverent comments about Roger Self and David Whitaker which I won't repeat here! Robert Watson, a fervent hockey fanatic and a member of the British Olympic Committee, bought some bottles of champagne for £140 each, but such was the celebratory mood that we all shook them up and sprayed each other. We were unaware of the cost at the time, but luckily Robert was pretty good natured and shrugged it off saying: 'Well, how often do your friends win gold medals?'

Many of the players drifted on to do their own thing once the dinner had finished. Some went to a disco, others went off with their wives and I joined Robert Clift and his parents and we went back to the family village. The bar had closed there but we managed to persuade them to open up and sell us a beer!

Steve Batchelor kept going back to his bed and looking at his medal, just to make sure it was still there and remind himself that we had really won.

2
WHERE IT ALL BEGAN

I was born on 24 September 1954 at Bromsgrove Cottage Hospital in Worcestershire. Although we lived in Kidderminster at the time, a town about 12 miles away, my mother had serious kidney problems which the local hospital couldn't cope with so we went to Bromsgrove. My sister, Christine, was nearly three when I was born but she suffered very badly from asthma and apparently because my father had spent a great deal of time looking after her, when I came along he informed my mother that I was all hers! But because my mother was still very ill she stayed on in hospital and I was taken home and looked after by my mother's sisters and brothers. She eventually had a kidney removed and visiting her in hospital many times is one of the lasting memories of my childhood.

My mother's maiden name was Bell and they were a very large and well-known family in Kidderminster. Her father was a master cabinet maker and her mother was a great lady who lived until she was 97. My father worked as a weaver at Victoria carpets in Kidderminster and eventually became a master weaver, weaving manager and then factory manager. Although he did well I think he was always a little bitter that the carpet industry never moved with the times and operated much as it had done for the previous thirty years, particularly by paying ridiculously low wages.

Whilst I obviously don't remember much about my early childhood, photographs reveal that I had blonde curly hair which is hard to believe now! I can recall fighting with my sister a lot and the story is told of how I ate a lump of coal just because she had told me not to. That probably explains why I have such a cast-iron stomach now, which is most beneficial when you're touring faraway countries! I know I teased her terribly but I suppose that's what all little brothers do. My primary school years are a little hazy but I went to Proud Cross school which was just around the corner, and in later years after we had moved, it was a pleasant walk down a hill. I used to hate history but I enjoyed maths and arts and crafts. Looking back on those days I can recall how grateful I was to the arts and crafts teacher who gave me such unlimited time and encouragement in something I enjoyed doing. I also loved all kinds of sport, but the only sport we had a chance to play at school was typical playground stuff – football, rounders and so on. By the time I got to my last year I was put 'in charge' of the juniors, and in my final summer term I helped organise a lot of games and I must say found it most enjoyable.

The main concern of the school was that traditions had to be kept, and passing the 11-plus was the most important objective for everyone. I duly passed and then had to make the decision about which grammar school to attend. There were two main choices – King Charles in Kidderminster which was bequeathed by King Charles to the people and maintained a variety of traditions, and Queen Elizabeth out in the countryside near Worcester in a village called Hartlebury. It was very difficult to get to but it had an aura about it which appealed to me. The boys who went to Queen Elizabeth seemed to have something special about them – indeed you had to have a bit of bottle to wear the uniform, which was a rather unconventional maroon colour and certainly made the pupils stand out in a crowd! Despite a lot of ribbing from my friends at King Charles, I actually became very proud of my school blazer and cap.

My sister and I were getting on better now and I was just beginning to share in her adulation of the Beatles and the loud pop music which constantly seemed to be blasting through the house. Christine was well established in her senior school and was always top of the class. At times I used to resent the pressure that was put on me by my parents throughout my schooling to try and match her high standards, because I was so keen on my sports and had far more to think about than an academic record.

Although my father didn't have much free time to play sport, I do remember going with him and my uncle to watch West Bromwich Albion regularly. It was almost a ritual and it carried on for a few years, from the times when I would sit on their shoulders, to when they took a stool for me up until I was tall enough to be able to see. My heroes in those days were the forwards Jeff Astle and Tony Brown, but despite having supported them all those years ago I'm not an avid fan these days – although I usually look for their results.

Every Sunday we used to go out in the car for a family outing, to Snowdonia or just up to the local hills. We'd either have a picnic lunch or go for a long ramble and come back for a big evening dinner, and it was a very important part of our lives. I'm sure one of the reasons we used to go to Wales was to help Christine's asthma although I probably didn't realise it at the time. Almost without fail whenever we were about half an hour from where we were going my mother would take out her hairspray and do her hair, which had the almost instant effect of making me violently carsick! I never had the heart to tell her that that was what caused it and for years the family believed that I would be carsick, on cue, about half an hour from our destination.

Occasionally I would go up to Kidderminster cricket club which was, and still is, used for some county games. I had a friend called Brian Pinner whose father was a very keen cricketer and we would take stumps and a bat and ball and have a game behind the pavilion. Brian had had some good coaching, and he invariably ended up batting all the time with me bowling to him – which is probably where my strength as a bowler developed.

My first competitive instincts unfolded when I started at Queen Elizabeth's. It was often a 'them' and 'us' situation with my friends, and I knew that I wanted to triumph. For the first time, I was really representing somebody. We were pitted against all the other local school teams at soccer, hockey and cricket. King Charles was much more of a rugby and athletics school, but I played against my old friends there too from time to time.

On the academic side, I always preferred the more precise subject such as maths and physics to subjects like French and English. I probably would have dropped history completely had it not been for my teacher, a Mr Hickman, who was very sympathetic and had a keen interest in cricket. The deputy headmaster, Mr Bartlet, was my maths teacher and he gave me lot of valuable direction when I left school and I have plenty to thank him for. I received a letter from him on my return from Seoul, which was a very nice touch because it was the first time we had been in contact for 17 years.

We had a system at the school which I abhorred, which was a sort of fagging organization which we were forced to be part of. Punishments included being thrown into the swimming pool on a freezing day, and being bombarded with snowballs. On one particular occasion, after being insolent to a prefect I was taken into the study and made to stand against the wall while he flicked a hockey ball all around my head. He never actually hit me but I remember it making a terrific noise as it rebounded around me. It was my first introduction to a hockey ball! I thoroughly enjoyed my first year, however, but the pressure told on me when the exams came round when I developed a slight nervous disorder through worrying about whether I was 'achieving' or not. Any difficulties I was having were purely due to laziness, as I couldn't discipline myself to do the homework and often ended up doing it on the bus going to school in the morning. I also found plain learning boring, and was quite content to put up with punishments rather than do it. Maths and science became my favourites.

The school was quite small, with only two hundred pupils and grounds set in rural Worcestershire farmland on top of a hill. Hartlebury village is a lovely little place and hasn't changed much except that the traditional grocers shop where I bought all my sweets seems to have made way for a big chain store. The school facilities were basic but well tended. We rolled the cricket square every lunchtime in the summer using a five-ton roller, and the football and hockey pitches were just lines marked out with posts stuck in. There was no indoor hall but we did have a tennis court and an outdoor, unheated swimming pool.

It was after school that all the fun started, and I hardly ever caught the bus straight home. It was then that we began all the cricket nets, practising in the goalmouth and improvising games. Very often I'd be there until it got dark. I would then have a frantic rush to make the six miles back home, and I was constantly reprimanded by my parents when I got in. We never had a specialised PE teacher at school and so much of our activity was spontaneous. When it was organised at school it would be supervised by a member of the academic staff, who would arrive in his suit and raincoat, with trousers tucked into a pair of socks or football boots. And if it was raining he would just add an umbrella! Cricket was much the same, and we learned by imitating the seniors. We certainly never had the benefit of professional coaching. Despite these short-comings we did produce several notable sportsmen including the goalkeeper David Owen who won nine England caps for hockey. Kevin Lucy, David Bridgford and I represented the county and the Midlands at football, cricket and hockey.

My first experience of hockey was in my second term at the school as an eleven-year-old when I joined in at a senior practice. I had started playing because it looked good fun. At that stage it was very much on the lines of playground football, with two jumpers thrown down as the goals and no definable boundaries. One of the lads who didn't know much about the game came in swinging his stick like Ballesteros, and hit me in the face knocking my two front teeth out. Mr Bartlet took me home, and I was rushed to hospital where I was then subjected to long and painful operations to repair the damage. It taught me the inherent dangers of playing with a piece of wood and a hard ball, and whenever I take beginners now I insist that they play with their hands wide apart in order to minimise the danger.

I continued to be successful in sports and varied my positions at hockey but I was definitely a goalkeeper in football. Strangely enough, I never had any ambition to be a wicketkeeper in cricket and only ever wanted to be the player who bowled people out. I thought I was a demon fast bowler but I suppose I was never much more than medium pace. In particular I enjoyed fielding, either in the covers or close to the bat. I think I held the school record for throwing the cricket ball until the school closed. It was 108 metres but I don't think I'd have a hope of achieving that now.

In my second season of hockey I was allowed to join in with the senior boys on occasions, and one day they asked me to stand in as goalkeeper. I put on the pads and kickers which were totally inadequate, never thought of a protective box, used the gloves and went out to face the star corner striker. His name was Radburn and he sent his first shot in. I can't remember if I saw it or not but it hit me straight between the eyes and down I went, absolutely pole-axed. Mr Bartlet drove me home again, and by that time I was regaining consciousness and began to vomit. So it was back in his car and off to hospital where I was diagnosed as having a fractured skull and was kept in for nearly a week. The headmaster came to see me and he advised me to never to play a game that I wasn't good enough at or adequately equipped for. I've never forgotten his advice.

When I returned I filled in again as a goalkeeper and from then on never looked back. I call recall sitting on the bus on the way home with my feet throbbing from all the shots I'd saved and generally suffering all over. I faced Radburn again and he didn't score! I believe he is still playing league hockey for Kidderminster club and scoring an abundance of goals.

As I continued to represent the school and shine, local clubs took an interest and so Saturday mornings became a mad race to play in school and club matches. As I got older it became even more hectic with the added attractions of girls and discos resulting in schoolwork slipping further down the list. My position in class dropped alarmingly and my parents put the brakes on my sport to encourage my academic leanings. I was determined to prove them wrong and that term came top in all my subjects! I didn't bother doing it again though.

At the age of 14 I was selected for my father's works' cricket team. They had a super ground which was well looked after and a man called Ken Stooke, a picking room manager in the factory, took me under his wing. He was an amazing cricket fanatic and was a member of the county club and the MCC. Ken used to spend hours talking to me about the game and how great bowlers held the ball, how they got it to turn and the attributes of class batsmen. He drove me everywhere and before long I was their main strike bowler. It was at this time that I began to field in the slips, and quite often I'd come away from a game having taken eight wickets and caught the other two in the slips!

I must confess the standard wasn't particularly high, but an important fixtures was always the local derby against another carpet manufacturer. I rushed back from school to play in it and after bowling our opponents out we needed four to win and I was batting. I hadn't batted for the previous few weeks and as I went in Ken said to me that we had plenty of overs to do it in, and that I should just have a look at the bowling and get them in singles. That was too much for me and I drove the first ball I faced straight back over the bowler's head for six! Ken was fuming that I had had the audacity to ignore him, but the other players thought it was tremendous and we had, after all, won the trophy.

If I admired any cricketers at that time they were Basil d'Oliveira and Norman Gifford, both of whom gave me good advice. I saw Basil hit five sixes in an over at the county ground once and as an impressionable schoolboy I thought that was brilliant, but Ken told me that that wasn't the way cricket should be played.

I'll always be grateful to my parents for the way they supported me during this time. My mother was little more than a glorified chauffeur at times, ferrying me around from match to match, while my father did his best to make sure I didn't drop the academic side completely! All in all, they certainly kept me on the straight and narrow by allowing me to exploit my natural instincts and interests. Nonetheless, I suppose sport did take precedence, and when I succeeded in passing 12 'O' Levels (three in the fourth year, the rest in the fifth), my father couldn't believe it!

I was now faced with having to decide which 'A' Levels to take. My thoughts went back to the dentist who had done such a good job when my teeth were knocked out. I remembered how pleasant he had been and, particularly, how rich he appeared! Dentistry would be what I would study and consequently I opted for chemistry, pure maths with statistics and biology. I figured that if it didn't work work then at least I had a few options open to choose from.

The one thing I could never work out at school was why exams always coincided with Wimbledon, the latest cricket series or the Olympic Games! I would be glued to these on the TV in between my own sports, and I recall rushing to watch the 1966 football World Cup. The strange thing about the World Cup was that although I was watching 'my' Bobby Charlton and 'my' Bobby Moore, my over-riding memory is of how stylish the Germans were. The first time I became aware of the Olympics was in 1968. The Games transfixed me with their almost supernatural aura which seemed totally out of my reach. It was watching the Olympics in 1968 which sowed the seed of my ambition. I never looked back.

When I turned 16, I decided that it was time to get a scooter. My parents were marvellous and my father and I went round at weekends to several garages in the area looking for the best one. Eventually we found my dream machine – a pearl white Lambretta SX 200 with metallic green flashes. I knew that I would be the envy of Kidderminster! The most important thing once we got it home was to get the L plates on and meet up with all my friends. About eight of us decided to go to Bridgnorth and visit a pub there. None of us would drink more than a half of bitter – the big thing was to be seen walking into a pub. Bridgnorth is an old picturesque town in Shropshire, built around a very steep hill. I coped quite well on the rather poor road surface and after we'd had our drink we came down a steep hill. The others went off quickly and I was left, as a learner, to negotiate the difficult descent. Unfortunately, I didn't take one corner terribly well and I drove straight into a wall. The next thing I knew, I was sitting on top of the wall, my dream scooter in a heap behind me. Some of my friends came rushing over with anxious looks on their faces and grabbed hold of me. Having ascertained that I was unhurt they pulled me down and only then did they tell me to turn round and see the huge drop below me that I could so easily have fallen down. I had to phone my father to come and collect me, and needless to say he was none too pleased about my escapade especially as the scooter was only eight hours old. Luckily one of my friends had the spare part necessary to repair, and before long I was back on the road.

My early pranks such as that incident were all part of making the transition from being a boy to a man, and although none of them were ever serious I certainly gave my parents worries. Certainly no pranks ever concerned malicious damage to other people's property, and really the worst I got up to was messing around on the scooter and irritating motorcyclists. I learned to dance, and at least girls proved to be a healthy distraction.

My cricket prospects improved when I was asked to go to selection games for the county senior level. I was also invited to a professional football trial at West Brom, where Don Howe was in charge at the time. I was accepted, but the terms I was offered as a goalkeeper were awful, and I felt that

I would probably do better to stick at my 'A' levels. I played in the county second cricket X1 and at that time they were playing in the competitive Birmingham league. The experience was good for me and I thoroughly enjoyed it, but it did reveal that I had a lot to learn.

Such a surfeit of sport was bound to catch up with me, and after one long cricket season I could hardly walk because of shin splints. I resorted to some gentle off-spin which didn't help, and my long recovery took me well into the autumn. It effectively ended my cricket career.

Having played county and Midland schoolboy hockey as well as representing the senior sides, I was invited to an England trial. My mother drove me down to St Albans and she stayed with a relative overnight. It was a real honour, quite unheard of in our area and my mother was a nervous wreck! The trials were a farce really and a lot depended on what you did when the selectors happened to be watching. I happened to make a couple of dramatic saves in front of them, which put me head and shoulders above everyone else.

I found the trials a daunting experience because most of the boys seemed to know one another and the public school tie was very much in evidence. I knew one, a lad called Steve Partington, who was an immensely talented player and the only person I'd met who could reverse flick the ball from the half-way line into the circle. He did that in the first game I played against him, flicking from the bully, which took me rather by surprise! Despite being very self-confident, I must admit that I felt frail and fragile in this environment because I didn't feel part of the system at all.

We gathered in the clubhouse afterwards, where my mother and aunt joined me. The chairman of the selectors stood up and announced the England team, and the first name he read out was mine. I could tell my mother was absolutely thrilled and I admired her self-restraint in the presence of what she considered 'well-to-do' people. There were several boys from schools such as Kingston Grammar, but the most interesting character was a 'scouser' who had an accent the likes of which I'd never heard before! He was a real prankster and entertained us for hours with the tricks he could do with a ball. Unfortunately he never came through the ranks and the last I heard of him he was deep into religion in the Far East.

My international debut was the home counties tournament at Winnington Park near Chester. My parents came up to watch. England were hot favourites and I let in a couple of silly goals, but also made numerous good saves and we won the tournament. It was the first time my father had seen me play and he enjoyed it so much that he became hooked from then on. Under my kickers in those days I used to wear an old pair of miner's boots that my father had acquired for me. They had enormous steel toe caps which enabled me to clear the ball a long way – but didn't do a lot for mobility!

Those first games in the schoolboy team started me off thinking how I could improve my game. Even though I was very nervous before the first match, I was immensely proud to wear the red rose and I still have it in a scrapbook somewhere. That was the start of my feelings of pride, and it was also the beginning of a yearning to be the best. I wanted to progress onwards and upwards, and I wasn't prepared to accept any second-rate achievement. To accommodate these objectives, I changed clubs to Stourport who I thought were a much more 'go-ahead' club, and we gradually went from the lower leagues to winning the Midlands championship.

Trips to training sessions at the national sports centre at Lilleshall became a way of life. I went there with Worcester-shire and Midlands schoolboys, under-23s and seniors as well as the England schoolboys, and it became almost a second home. One year I worked out that I must have spent something like 23 weekends at the national sports centre. I got to know the staff extremely well – particularly those in the kitchen!

All this hockey was slowly throttling my enthusiasm for cricket, since I had little time for anything else, and at the end of my last summer at school I had only played a few games. My school days drew to a close and when the 'A' Level results came out, I didn't attain good enough grades to go to the medical school in Birmingham. My parents were disappointed but what they didn't realise was that I had actually lost the desire to be a dentist. I then had to make the decision about what career path I would follow.

It was my old friend Mr Bartlet who asked me if I had ever thought about being a school teacher. We mulled over the idea and decided that going to a physical education college would dovetail perfectly with my aspirations in sport. There was the choice of Loughborough, St Luke's in Exeter or Borough Road in London. I elected to go to London without hesitation because that was where all the top hockey players were based. I was invited to go for an interview and spoke to Jimmy Biddle who was head of the PE department and also manager of the British athletics team at the time. I got on well with him and was offered a place to do a B.Ed in physical education and natural sciences.

I was tremendously excited at the thought of being in London and getting involved in college life. What impressed me there was the standard of all the other students and I felt quite humble about my own achievements. There were schoolboy international athletes, rugby players and cricketers. Simon Rodhurst, the reigning shot-putting champion, was there and his dedication and hard work was something I shall never forget. He used to get me to help him with his training and I would sit on his back while he did his numerous press-ups. Sadly he was killed in a road accident just after we had both made our senior international debuts. The Leicestershire cricketer Nigel Briers was in my year, Phil Bainbridge of Gloucestershire was a year below me and Brian Rose, another professional, captained the college cricket team. We had a very strong side and in the three years I played for the college team all our fixtures were against county second sides. I was the only one in the side who wasn't signed up by a county, and most of them have since gone to carve out successful careers on the professional county cricket scene.

It was difficult to excel in such illustrious company and I found myself being well beaten at sports like cross country, swimming and the javelin. (I had once taken part in an England schoolboys javelin trial but was soundly thrashed by David Ottley who went on to win a silver medal at the Los Angeles Olympics!) Such defeats brought home to me my inadequacies and stopped me from getting too big for my boots.

I never did join a London hockey club during my college days, but continued to travel back and represent Stourport. Graham Sayers, who was a good friend of mine from the club, was working in London and we used to share the journeys either going back on Friday evenings or first thing Saturday morning. For much of the season that was how I spent my weekends. Stourport and Worcestershire went from strength to strength and one season I can remember only letting in three goals at club level.

I decided that whilst I was at college I would have a go at as many sports as possible to make up for all the years I had never had a PE teacher at school. I learnt to pole-vault with Brian Hooper, and a chap called Keith Atkins taught me how to high jump. I shared a house at the time with Andy Whittle, who was an England under-21s rugby player, and Elgan Rees from Wales, and so I took up rugby which was great. In my final year we had a real international household with Nigel Briers, Elgan Rees and a fencer whose name escapes me. It was a typical bachelors' haunt with jockstraps and dirty laundry all over the place and a fridge that was always empty! We used to get drunk and eat badly and do all the usual sorts of things that students do.

By now I had won an international under-23s cap and we played Young Holland, a Japanese team and also Sweden. Six of the Swedes held their sticks the wrong way round and back to front so that they were always playing on the reverse stick side and hitting the ball with the back of their sticks. I think that was the influence of ice hockey, but we beat them 8–0 at Crystal Palace.

In my last year at college I made the decision that the Olympics were the key thing to aim for. That was what everyone talked about, that was what mattered and that was the sportsman's dream. I gave up drinking and began an intensive training programme. The video facility at college was to prove invaluable in helping me analyse my technique. Whenever people asked me what it was all in aid of and why I was doing it, I replied that I was going to win an Olympic gold medal.

Apparently even when I went home I used to tell people that this was my burning ambition, and lots of them have reminded me of this since I returned from Seoul. An old farmer friend, George Wheeler, tells the story of how when he was giving me lift back from Stourport one day I told him that I was going to win the gold medal. To achieve this I had to be the best and to be the best was going to require a special dedication but I was prepared to set out on this path. I also figured that what set two individuals of equal ability apart was style, and I resolved that I would create a unique style of goalkeeping.

My first teaching practice was at Dulwich College where Alan Pascoe, the Olympic hurdler, was a teacher. I covered for him while he was at the Commonwealth Games, and my stint was extended because he was away for something like nine weeks which seemed quite incredible to me – particularly as I only took off two weeks for the World Cup! I gained a good insight into teaching and also realised what a drag it was to have to commute on the underground from the other side of London to get there every morning. I spent another teaching practice at Tiffins Boys School in Kingston, which was primarily a rugby-playing school with great emphasis on academic achievement. By this stage Alan Pascoe had returned to the college as a lecturer and he came to assess my final teaching practice. It was interesting to note the instant esteem in which I was held when I walked into the staff room with him. That esteem was something that no hockey player could have inspired at the time – it taught me a lot about how people regard different sports.

To this day I still recall how poor wages were for teachers and I used to wonder why on earth I wanted to be a school teacher. I love the children and being with them, but I have always hated inadequacies in my colleagues and the pettiness in the staff room. I must admit that I was never strongly attached to the idea of teaching but it fitted in with my ambition at the time, and allowed me to the freedom to practise my sport. A career wasn't important at that stage of my life. Because I wasn't brave enough to get out of it, teaching was convenient – particularly as public shools regarded it as prestigious to have an international on the staff. Looking back it was a remarkably shortsighted view for me to take.

I think it is fair to say that when I came to the end of my college days I realised that I had gained very little from the course on either the physical education or the academic side. It failed to instil much enthusiasm in me and certainly hadn't inspired me to any great heights. But I had loved meeting such a variety of friends and I learnt a lot about attitudes and correct procedures on the 'phys-ed' side.

We had a tremendous college hockey team and I remember Elgan Rees played on the wing and Nigel Briers was on the left. We conscripted a football goalkeeper, I played right-half and we had Gary Doer, a junior European triple jumper, at centre-forward. He was certainly the fastest man I'd ever seen and his nickname was 'deer'. He would pick up all the long passes, streak past defenders and touch the ball in the net. We lost 2–1 to the powerful Southgate side in the Cup that year, which was a fantastic achievement because they were the reigning European Champions. Included in their team were David Whitaker and Bernie Cotton – coach and assistant respectively of the gold medal squad in Seoul. The most intricate problem we had to deal with was hiring the minibus to take us to games. Inevitably one member of the side was coerced in to persuading the hire company that one of us was over 25 and somehow 'in charge'!

Cricketing days were equally enjoyable. I'll never forget the British Colleges final that was played at Chiswick one year. Our opening pair, Nigel Briers and Mike McEvoy, put on 60-odd and we required something like 98 to win the limited overs match. They batted in the classic opening fashion and I went in when Mike was out and hit two fours and four sixes to finish the game in flamboyant style! Nigel offered to help arrange terms for me at Leicestershire and I declined, but I often wonder now if perhaps I should have accepted and how it would have all worked out.

I then felt that I was in superb cricketing form and was full of confidence, but the next game quickly brought me back down to size! We played Middlesex second X1 and John Emburey, who was captain, had me caught second ball at leg slip. Nigel went on to make a superb score after a patient and workman-like start. His most impressive shot was when he pulled Emburey over mid-wicket for six and it went right over the college itself – which is a five storey building – and lost the ball! From then on I realised what being a professional is all about and what attitude is required to be successful. I was gleaning information from other sports all the time from the psychological point of view, in order to help me do well in hockey.

During my college holidays I used to take on various jobs to try and earn a bit of pockey money. I made friends with a chap called Chris Dark and at the end of my first summer we went down to the M23 which was being built to Brighton, and got a variety of construction jobs. They paid enormous sums for those days. I think my first term's grant was £110, but my labouring jobs earned me £160 a week, which was more than my father was earning at the time! I saved up enough to buy a sports car to impress my friends at college. The first summer I bought a Triumph Spitfire, and the second time a Triumph GT6 which had a two-litre engine with overdrive and was the fastest car I'd ever driven. It was a bit swish! Another year I worked underneath the Gatwick terminal, building a pumping station 40 feet underground. It didn't take me too long to realise that working that distance below ground level with several Irishmen who spent their lunchtimes drinking and then drove fork-lift trucks could result in serious consequences!

Once I left college I had to find a job, and as luck would have it, Tiffins School informed me that they had a vacancy. I'll always remember my interview because one of the other candidates was Rowley Brookeman who was the current England and Great Britain hockey right-wing. Here I was, a junior international competing with an established senior one, in a non-hockey school. After my second interview I was so convinced that Rowley would get the post that I never even thought to worry about it. Naturally, I was surprised and thrilled to accept the position when it was offered to me around tea-time.

I found some accommodation with another member of staff called Dave Crowther (he also wrote to me on my return from Seoul) who had a bachelor flat in a place called Grange Mansions just outside Kingston. I spent a couple of years there, and because I was a young teacher trying to save money, the heating wasn't on much, there was never much food and it was probably only slightly more sophisticated than being a student. His mother used to come round once a fortnight and dust and polish, and Dave was kind and obliging and we had some fun together.

In my first year of teaching I joined Slough hockey club. In one particular match against Beckenham, the top side at that stage, I played an absolute blinder, saved two penalty strokes and denied some of their seasoned internationals countless scoring opportunities. We won the match, which was quite unheard of. After a few more good matches I was invited to an England training weekend at Bishop's Stortford College. Many of the seniors didn't even speak to me because I was considered a youngster, and I vowed there and then I would never, under any circumstances, do that when I was in their position. I felt reasonably pleased with my showing and from there I went on to win the national clubs title with Slough, then the London League, and went into the European Cup with them.

One day my parents left a message at Grange Mansions for me to 'phone home immediately. When I spoke to them they said there was a letter for me from the Hockey Association which I asked them to open. It informed me that I had been selected to represent England in a Six Nations Tournament in Amsterdam. My parents were delighted and I was thrilled that I had achieved an important objective. My international career had begun.

3
THE GOALKEEPING CHALLENGE

When I began to keep goal at school, I adopted what were the accepted goalkeeping methods in those days. It was only really through my college days that I came to realise that just doing what someone else had done before wasn't necessarily the way to become the best. It was whilst I was at college, and meeting a wide range of top sportsmen, that I really started to analyse the requirements of my game. I studied all the renowned players, breaking down the strengths and weaknesses of each and matching them up against what I considered to be required. I did this in the form of a study on goalkeeping using photographic analysis and psychological input to reach my final conclusions.

After this study at college, I took it upon myself to revolutionise the goalkeeper's cumbersome equipment in order to facilitate the new techniques I was developing. My main concern was that all international goalkeepers prior to me had worn canvas pads. These didn't fit in with the style that I was hoping to develop, because the majority of saves I wanted to make would be with the side the leg and many of the old techniques required the shinbone to be kept facing the ball.

To solve this I needed to find something else that suited me and I looked to the continental pad. I didn't want to adopt the continental style in itself, but rather to be able to develop and modify their pad to fit in with my own ideas which were a mixture of the two styles.

In the same way I decided to modify the kickers and boots which were then being worn. I needed to be much quicker and more agile in the circle and it was important to get away from the old miner's boots! I worked with a goalkeeping friend in developing a new kicker, which was a wedge-like shape made of modern materials and without a metal protective cap, in order to make it light. The style became quite popular, and when England toured India in 1977 the England goalkeeper John Hurst and I talked about this at length. The basic concept was that a goalkeeper is a mobile person, and not an immovable object placed between the ball and the goal. A firm was set up in the Midlands to manufacture the new kicker, which became known as the SE Mason kicker.

The second concern of my study was that whatever force was put into a shot at goal should be used effectively to redirect the ball. I think a good analogy is a cricket one: where goalkeepers previously played a forward defensive, now they were playing a drive. John Hurst and I spent endless hours modifying the pads using needle and thread, bits of foam and anything we thought could help. We basically developed a continental-style pad but with a rebound material in it, and a light wedge-shaped kicker that had high rebound properties. There were several deficiencies, and inevitably we suffered awful bruising in practice from time to time.

The gloves available in England at that time were terrible and provided little protection against the powerful shots we were continually having to save. In my early days as an international, I went to Germany and incorporated the Erhard gloves which existed over there into my equipment. Even as internationals we had to buy these gloves in from Germany at £100 a pair in 1977, but at the time they were the best on the market. John and I also spent time with the stick, and busied ourselves with files, saws and sandpaper.

We decided to try and achieve maximum width and lightness for flicking and stopping ability. We didn't consider hitting to be part of a 'keeper's repertoire, and therefore decided that the head of the stick needn't carry too much weight.

There was enough there to take a long time to develop and although later on there were further improvements with helmets, shoulder and chest pads, really we had come a long way since wearing a pair of pads, t-shirt, box, gloves and kickers. It was during this period in 1977 that I took over as first choice 'keeper, and when John was taken ill with dysentery in India I seized the opportunity to make it my position. This tour was the first time the save-clear technique was seen on the international circuit.

Our side wasn't particularly strong and I was kept busy, but I wanted to get my techniques accepted. On such an intensive tour I had the chance to practise hour by hour to develop my technique, and I would assert my authority at these practices to perfect it. I could tell different players what I wanted them to do, explaining that I was trying to use any power that they were putting into the shot to propel the ball away. I felt that a goalkeeper should control the defence, and that although goalkeepers might not be involved for long periods of time it was the manipulation of the defenders by the person who had the best view that would lead to success.

My performances backed up my word concerning the change in the emphasis of control. I made the right saves at the right time, which helped people to accept me telling them what to do.

I think what sparked me off on the theme of clearing a ball rather than just stopping it was when I watched Peter Mills in goal for England against West Germany at Lord's. He made a brilliant save from a fierce drive by a German attacker and all the German did then was pick it up and push the ball in to the net. Goal! Why bother with a brilliant save? Why not let the first one go straight in? The problem with goalkeepers preceding my era was that rebounds were being scored and 'keepers were stopping the ball and not clearing it very well, which gave attackers two or three opportunities from the same situation. My technique, therefore, was whenever possible to get the ball back beyond the forwards, out of the circle and if possible, initiate a counter attack.

In terms of my own limitations, I had to work out where to put my ankle or my knee in order to clear the ball. Sometimes the ball would squirt out the side and sometimes it would go straight back to the forward. Much of what I was trying to do was quite logical in theory, but in practice there were times when it had an adverse effect on the team, because they were used to responding to a ball at the 'keeper's feet or which had just been stopped. We worked on the basic reflection principle, that the angle of incidence equals the angle of reflection. The important thing was how the other players responded to a shot coming in, having to get used to the ball coming in in one direction and going out in another. There were some amusing incidents when they weren't sure in which direction the ball was going to be cleared, and some defenders received a few hard shots on the backs of their legs!

Canvas pads would now serve little useful purpose, and in came the cane pads which were already being used on the Continent. These incorporated the high density foam and plastics that were now available. The use of high density foams combined in little packages or sandwiches in the right areas have helped to create the style in use today. It's now possible to clear the ball well over the halfway line owing to the speed of the initial shot and the rebound quality of the material used. Control is the key element in directing the rebound, and goalkeepers are required to concentrate extremely hard. I must admit that I received an enormous amount of co-operation from players in England and in the national squad, and I would frequently practise this clearing technique with my team-mates.

I returned from India full of confidence, convinced that I was now the first choice goalkeeper. Selection for the 1978 World Cup in Buenos Aires was imminent, and I hoped that I would be chosen to go. I was still pretty inexperienced on the international scene and I wasn't sure what to expect. Artificial surfaces were becoming popular and I wondered how my technique would fare on a plastic pitch, although the World Cup was still played on grass. I was duly selected for the squad and before we left we played a couple of internationals at Lord's. We beat India 2–1 and then lost heavily 5–3 to Australia with a chap called Rowan Dick scoring all five. Two of our defenders were definitely not up to standard and were incapable of performing at that level. Dick certainly gave me a lesson in how to score goals, and I learnt a lot all round from that experience.

Due to that convincing victory over us by Australia, however, I was dropped for the opening match of the World Cup – which coincidentally was against the Australians – and John Hurst was preferred in goal. After that match I came back in, and we had a mixture of results. I managed to keep the German corner striker Wolfgang Strodter out, and in those days the rule didn't require the ball to hit the backboard first. Picking the ball out of the air was one of my strong points. I was awarded the title 'Best Goalkeeper of the Tournament' by the hockey writers, and was written about as the best goalkeeper in the world. I remember thinking that I wanted to keep that title for the rest of my playing career. I was particularly pleased that I had succeeded ahead of Martin Sikking, the legendary Dutch 'keeper, who still used the 'old' method of stopping the ball first. He was quite unique in that he held the stick in his left hand, had a special glove made for his right hand and always cleared the ball using the reverse stick.

The advent of artificial pitches completely changed the game. In April 1979 we travelled to a tournament in Perth where an artificial surface was used. It was the first time we had played on such a surface, and in fact was one of the earliest tournaments to be staged on one. Crystal Palace was the only pitch in England that we could prepare on, which was obviously more of a football pitch although it sufficed for training purposes. We had to go out on January mornings in below-zero temperatures – quite unsuitable as preparation for the hockey that we would be playing in a vast concrete stadium in heat reaching 35°C! But it was one of the tournaments necessary for Great Britain to be sure of qualification for the 1980 Olympics in Moscow. We had to do well.

It was a difficult time for me because I had set my own standards for what I wanted to do in goalkeeping and the manager, Roger Self, asked a former international 'keeper, Harry Cahill, to come along and give me some coaching. I found it impossible to do most of the things he was asking me to do as they weren't relevant to my game. He was impressed with my kicking, and found it hard to believe that I had developed a kicker which enabled me to put a ball onto the walkway at Crystal Palace from ground level with nonchalant ease. After half a day he told Roger that it was pointless carrying on, because of the totally different techniques that I was using.

The development of the game on artificial surfaces meant distinct adjustments for the goalkeeper. Clearing the ball out of the circle meant a constant metamorphosis of style as the ball travelled even quicker across the circle. An interesting feature of the the Perth tournament was the incredibly high scores achieved all round. This was because forwards found it so much easier to get past defenders. Previously, attackers had been stopped by slow, bumpy pitches and they would also rely on another forward running with them to receive the pass. Now, the incredible speed of the ball across the artificial surface meant that strikers could beat the defenders who hadn't yet utilised the low indoor style of tackling. Once a forward was level with the defence they were as good as beaten, because by the time they had turned, the forward had a four- or five-yard start. On grass the ball would be slowed down considerably.

The number of goals scored was not only due to this factor, but also due to the lack of technique in the early days. Often there were scores of 7–5, 6–4 and it was exciting end-to-end action. Goalkeepers tended to be kept very busy and would be led a merry dance all round the circle by forwards relishing the friendly nature of the surface. I remember the Australian striker Terry Walsh in the bar after one of our games, doing a supposed radio commentary of a World XI taking on a Pakistan XI who were then the masters. It went like this: 'And now they're in the circle and here's Taylor and he saves and now he's up and he dives and he's down and he saves and he's up and he's across and he saves and he turns round and he's down and . . . it's a goal!' That summed up perfectly the frustrations of a goalkeeper under those conditions!

A good example of the gradual improvement in defensive techniques is shown in the bronze medal match of the 1984 Olympics when Great Britain met Australia. The Australians had 33 penalty corners and 47 attempts on goal to Great Britain's three penalty corners. We won the match 3–2, which I think indicates a remarkable performance by the British defenders and shows how far we had progressed since those early days on plastic pitches – although there were of course weaknesses in the Australian side.

Britain had a side of mixed ability, some at the end of their careers and others who were looking ahead to the future. Several members still played for pure enjoyment and although they wanted to win, winning was never a foremost objective in their mind. It's also fair to say that some of them just went along for the ride. It was an attitude that I found difficult to comprehend. At the end of the tournament I felt I had done well and once again, I was honoured to be recognized as the outstanding goalkeeper.

By the 1980s most goalkeepers had switched to 'my style' of equipment, with skeleton pads and high rebound kickers. Others went over to a more subdued skeleton-style pad without the rebound qualities, and a box continental kicker which was very square and tended to stop a ball dead. This feature is something I don't agree with because anything that has a false platform under your feet has got to be bad, and something that doesn't allow you to play on the balls of your feet is equally inferior. If you observe any tennis player it's easy to notice how they move on the balls of their feet, and good goalkeeping follows the same principle. Nonetheless this box kicker remains popular and is widely used today.

When we withdrew from the 1980 Moscow Olympics, which I'll expand on later, I was not only extremely disappointed but was also very angry. I had earned the reputation as the world's best goalkeeper, my new style was working and my ambition to win a gold medal had been dashed. At the end of that year we moved into a new generation of hockey players, with talented young players like Richard Dodds and Richard Leman coming through. I felt like quite a seasoned international as by this stage I had played in the European Cup, the World Cup and the Champions' Trophy, and won everything there was to win with my club, both at home and in Europe. Although I was still changing my ideas and style, I did it much less frequently and I was now seriously looking at which direction my career was going to take. I decided I'd had enough of being an 'also ran', sitting in the stands during presentation ceremonies. I felt that we had the right up-and-coming players to be successful (including a young centre-forward called Sean Kerly) and was determined to continue in my quest for the top.

We got several things wrong with the tournaments in this period of development. There was a domestic crisis when Southgate representatives decided not to go to the European Cup because of their club commitments, and we had the added problems of trying to blend together a new side as well as adapting our game to the novel surface. Despite the withdrawal of the Southgate players, England managed to finish fifth but it was a downward trend compared with our bronze medal in 1978.

The 1982 World Cup was held shortly after Christmas in Bombay, where the unbearable heat and humidity was destined to take a terrible toll on the players. If we had been better prepared we would have flown out on about the 20th December, but as it turned out we left after Christmas which gave us less than two days until our first match. The combination of jet lag, heat and lack of preparation meant we finished a disappointing ninth.

This was an interim period, however, and although certain individual reputations fluctuated, the important point was that we were building a team. Some people felt that my displays weren't as impressive as they should have been, but in actual fact I probably made just as many good saves as I was able. The problem was that as a young team we were exposed on a surface which was betraying any teams that lacked either in physical ability or experience. We could only perform well if everyone was on form, and the effectiveness of our defence was dependent on how well the forwards were doing their job up front – when and where they gave the ball away and when and where they kept possession.

The penalty corner began to prove more and more crucial on the new surface, both because of the speed the ball could now be hit across the circle, and also because corner strikers moved in four or five yards to shoot. It hadn't always been possible to do this on grass. Goalkeeping weaknesses were being highlighted and two international 'keepers, a German and the Soviet Vladimir Pleshakov, began lying down to defend them simply because they felt they hadn't got the reaction time. They mixed standing up and lying down, creating a different technique that was to prove most effective. I still strongly resisted it and always cited the German 'keeper who tried the method during a tour of Australia in 1982 but was so badly injured by a shot that he later had a testicle removed.

With incidences like that continuing to happen, I was determined to continue with my own style of standing up and using my reactions to stop the shot. Unfortunately, I worked on the principle that the goal was narrower by two feet or one foot six, because I could always rely on the outer nine inches being defended by fullbacks on the line. But in time, of course, we lost those people like Mike Corby and Bernie Cotton who had the exceptional ability to defend those precious nine inches. With shots coming in so much faster, I rapidly had to rethink how I was going to cope with this interesting problem.

In 1983 we went on a tour of Australia. We ended up beating the Australians, which was excellent because they were an extremely strong force to be reckoned with at the time. My technique of standing up continued to prove successful and I received the accolade of best goalkeeper in the world. The strength of our team was shown in our unity and not any one individual, and as we set out to Hong Kong in 1983 to qualify for the Los Angeles Olympics we were filled with confidence. Great Britain had to finish in the top three to do it, and we thought that perhaps even fourth would suffice. Certainly if we could do better than Malaysia, who were our main rivals for the place, then we were home and dry.

During all this time I continued to pursue my dream of the Olympics. I felt satisfied that I would have made the grade when Moscow staged the Games, and believed therefore that my golden opportunity was about to present itself. As I was about 28 or 29 at the time, there were also odd thoughts crossing my mind that I could be coming to the end of my career. It was at the Hong Kong tournament, when the Australian Craig Davies struck three corner goals between the full-back and the post, that I realised that something had to be done about my technique. Perhaps I should start lying down after all. I was also very hurt because Roger Self, the manager, made me the scapegoat for the team's poor showing and suddenly my confidence disappeared. I thought it was rather poor personnel management.

Britain came fourth in the tournament and Malaysia fifth. After a protracted meeting, the international governing body invited Malaysia to the Olympics. I'm convinced that it was a political decision but there were also three other teams in Europe ranked higher than us and on the strength of that we were excluded. I heard of the decision on the way back home and my world fell apart. Not only had my technique supposedly faltered at corners, but my sporting career appeared to be devastated. I must confess that I hadn't shown my best form, but the failings of the squad were not the failings of the goalkeeper.

The weaknesses of standing up were becoming more apparent, but I was still certain that my method shouldn't be discarded. I considered that I had been given a raw deal, and forgot about international hockey for a couple of months. I brooded over the decision not to invite Britain to Los Angeles and wondered whether I was ever going to win my gold medal. It was a low period for me. My anguish was short-lived however, when I heard that the Soviets had withdrawn from the Olympics and, as first reserves, Britain was invited to step in with only a few months remaining. Luckily I had been playing and was enjoying life with a new club, East Grinstead. We had won several titles and were going into Europe for the European Cup. Suddenly, it was get ready for the Games!

I was still at the crossroads as far as my goalkeeping was concerned. I was determined that the upright technique was still superior. My colleague in the side, Veryan Pappin, had adopted the horizontal Soviet style and was promoting it and the manager, Roger Self, insisted that I adopt this technique. There were several warm-up matches as part of our preparation, but I still refused to lie down for a number of reasons. Firstly there was that of safety. The equipment that people were using was totally inadequate, particularly to protect the upper body and abdomen, and was therefore dangerous. The chest protectors weren't made to withstand shots fired in at 100 miles per hour. There was little or no protection for the arms, and the face masks available at the time were useless. I was vindicated for a short while at least when, whilst on a pre-Olympic tour in Europe, we played two games against Holland. They scored three penalty corner goals against Veryan in one game to win 3–0, and I said to Roger that if I let in a corner goal in the match the following day then I would consider changing my technique. We drew 0–0 and I survived about 12 penalty corners! It's worth mentioning that both of us had two on the line.

When we arrived in Los Angeles, however, Roger still insisted that I use some sort of lying-down technique and he eventually issued me with an ultimatum. Either I adjusted or he didn't play me. It was madness with little over a week to go, but we eventually reached a compromise. As I couldn't stomach the thought of lying there like a sack of potatoes waiting to be hit, I suggested approaching penalty corners as an open play situation. I would take the man on and block the shot, but to do that I would need far superior equipment. Roger agreed that if I could purchase what I needed then I should do so. We went to a professional ice rink, and in the shop there bought a helmet, chest pads, shoulder pads, special shorts, abdomen guard and double box. I went out to practise and tried the gear out. The helmet was very difficult to get used to because I had never worn one before, and so I only wore it for those corners where I knew that I wouldn't be able to determine whether the ball would hit me in the face or not. Practices went well, although I had to put up with an awful lot of aches and pains since the equipment I was wearing was designed for ice hockey and not for extending the arms in any way. I received an enormous amount of painful blows under my arms, on my hip bone and between the shorts and the hockey pads, which are a different height to ice hockey pads.

The revised method was fairly simple, and I always adhered to the philosophy of attacking the ball. I would sprint off my line at a corner and spread myself in front of the striker, trying to throw my knees through the line of the ball and cover all of the goal by the time the ball was hit. I was careful to adhere to the basic principles of goalkeeping that I had always used, and was aware that what I what I was doing was a 'one-off' to comply with a unique situation. Of course another reason for the innovative method was that the FIH rule change in the early 1980s made it necessary for the ball to hit the backboard (which is about 18 inches high) with the initial shot at goal. The inefficiency of the full-backs on the line made it necessary to spread oneself to create a horizontal barrier, and led to the popularisation of this style of 'keeping.

I put my novel method into serious practice in a match we played against the Australians two days before the Games began, and it worked rather well. To be fair, I only defended about six corners but they didn't score, and since they weren't in our pool anyway no one paid much attention to what I was doing. Everyone in our camp seemed pleased with the way we had performed, and I was confident that I could take on the best in the world. We went into our first match against Kenya full of optimism.

At their first penalty corner the Kenyans chipped the ball straight down the middle, it hit me on the top of my pad and shot into the roof of the goal. That shattered absolutely everything because if I had remained standing up it would have come straight to me and I probably would have cleared it over the halfway line! This 'flying bedspread' method developed through those Olympic Games and certainly hadn't been formulated or coached by anybody prior to Los Angeles. By the time we got through to the final stages Neil Snowdon, the Australian, had begun to try it and the Dutch 'keeper mixed it with other techniques, but the Pakistanis and Indians remained standing. The Asians, particularly Pakistan who were the World Champions, continued without change in their traditional way.

On my return from Los Angeles I deduced that the technique was far too easily taken advantage of. This was illustrated in the semi-finals when West Germany beat us 1–0. They worked a clever switch at a corner, and by playing the ball square twice moved me something like twenty yards and stopped the ball in front of goal behind me, leaving one of their players the simple task of smashing in the winner. It was a perfectly executed indoor move. My method of overcoming this was not to rush out to the circle edge but rather achieve a compromise between the two styles. I began to think how best to save a ball in the air – whether I should let it drop or not, what to do if the ball switched about and what to do if the ball was flicked. I'm discussing these options here in order to emphasise how the specialities of the position change all the time. If a goalkeeper misses a major tournament, therefore, he could be letting himself in for a great deal of trouble. I always insisted on attending all the tournaments I was selected for, because the game is developing so rapidly that I wouldn't have been able to adjust my style to suit the progress in the game if I missed out on any.

The pace of development has been on going ever since. When I started in club games again after the Olympics I only used the horizontal position in one event, because I was generally confident in my ability to prevent the shot without doing so. I knew I could face Sean Kerly and Paul Barber quite easily but in certain situations, without the support of the right full-backs and with the closeness that some strikers were approaching, it's necessary to try everything to put an opponent off! The more options you force a striker to take, the less likely he'll be to score, because he'll be in two minds before he shoots. By then, hopefully, it'll be too late!

It's worth mentioning that in 1979 I played in the semi-final of the Esanda tournament against Australia in Perth, and in that tournament they had 34 penalty corners and scored one. In Los Angeles, as I've said before, they had 33 and again scored one. In these two tournaments I had used completely different techniques, on exactly the same surface and opposing equally competent strikers. In fact, Craig Davies probably did most of the shooting in both of them, which clearly shows the effectiveness of both of these contrasting styles. A good 'keeper alone could not keep up that record, which demonstrates how essential an efficient defensive team is. The important factor is how well the defence and goalkeeper combine.

Following on from the bronze medal we won in Los Angeles, I set myself further objectives. It was becoming more and more difficult to achieve them, however, owing to my family commitments and the fact that I wasn't getting any younger. I'd always wanted the title 'the best in the world', and I was determined to keep it. Having made the decision to carry on playing, the next objective was the World Cup in London in 1986. Two aims were uppermost in my mind: the first was to continue as the best goalkeeper in the world, and the second was to be in the England side that became World Champions.

We took part in a Champions' trophy before the World Cup, and it was fascinating to watch several goalkeepers rushing out and paying the price for it. Most teams now had goalkeepers employing some form of horizontal style, and there continued to be lively debates about this technique. The Dutch and other continental sides dropped a yard from the line with the intention of killing the ball dead, but the Pakistanis and Indians would rush out at the ball like I did in 1984. I revised my technique and combined the best features of both. Our defensive tactics would be that whichever side the ball was pushed out from, the number one person would run out with the objective of putting off or closing down the striker of the ball. The second and third runners would primarily cover the goalkeeper, because he was stretched out in front of as much of the goal that he could block. One runner would clear any shot of the 'keeper's legs, and the other man would protect the head side. But more likely he would sweep away any danger that arose from a ball that had been half hit into the keeper's body and which was sure to be picked up by forwards rushing in to score from the rebound. This person was also certain to be an excellent reader of the options and would defend situations where the ball was worked around the circle.

I must admit that this pattern was never really rigidly stuck to, and we would change our defensive tactics according to each new situation that arose. If you are so predictable that you can state exactly where you'll be in each circumstance, then you are predictable enough to be beaten. It is the adaptation and unpredictability in any goalkeeper that makes him or her great.

I know that I could always successfully distract the West German Carsten Fischer, who strikes from the top of the circle, by moving much further off my line, in the region of the penalty spot, towards him. John Bestall from Australia likes to squeeze down on the ball, and with him I would stay back in order to catch the ball as it came down from its arc. If I had rushed out to him, the chances would be that the ball would have gone over me and I would have been beaten. If a player didn't hit the ball quite as hard then obviously I would hang back and save the shot as it came in, and anything unexpected would be dealt with by the two men next to me. In the Olympic final I think I won the psychological battle with Carsten, because by being unpredictable he was always in two minds and was constantly undecided as to which option to take.

I was very satisfied with my play during the World Cup in 1986 and it was only occasionally, through error of judgements, that corner goals were scored. In the semi-final against West Germany, Carsten Fischer occasionally did squeeze one past me, but that was because it was their fifteenth of 17 corners and the whole defence was beginning to tire. I was slow to get my elbow in to the right position and the ball went in off my forearm. I began to feel after Willesden that too much emphasis was being placed on this horizontal technique and that goal-keepers were neglecting the basics of vertical goalkeeping. I found that I was adopting horizontal moves in open play situations when they were completely unnecessary. Forwards were becoming accomplished at chipping and lifting a ball on the run to beat a prone 'keeper, and they were also very adept at forcing the 'keeper to go down and then moving the ball away and flicking it over him.

Post-1986 I was convinced that I had the mental attitude and in the physical ability to set my sights toward Seoul and the gold medal that had eluded me for so long. Several of the Stourport players like Godfrey Lamb and some of the junior internationals patiently helped me practise, and we would spend hours at the Perdiswell Centre in Worcester trying out a variety of ideas. I worked exclusively on what I call 'good hockey habits for a goalkeeper' which, in essence, was good vertical technique.

Corresponding with that was the development of equipment, and with all the interest that was now being shown in the game I was able to use the resources available to help my ideas. I tried out the different high-density foams and carried on developing kickers, but unfortunately it is a slow process and some of the equipment has taken years to get right. If I was doing it professionally I could probably do it in a week but the difference is that you play, try it, send it back, and six weeks later it comes back and so it goes on. Chest pads should not be made of high-density foams because this material tends to compress, which can be very painful for a 'keeper. I came up with a material with the Stafford Rubber Company which was an expanded high density foam that had set solid. These chest pads, combined with ice hockey shoulder pads and extra protection of my arms and forearms, gave me an adequate defence.

The helmet I now use was also adopted from ice hockey, with a visor that I feel least restricts my vision. Some goalkeepers wear a neck flap to protect their Adam's apple, but personally I've always believed that good technique relies on your chin being down and your head weight being kept forward. Your throat should therefore never be exposed even at penalty corners. I wear a cricket abdomen guard and then an ice hockey one which is extra 'just in case', and on top of all that a pair of ice hockey shorts which have built-in thigh, hip and kidney guards. The cane pads are still the best but instead of kapok stuffing there are now water-resistant, water-repellant, high-density but very low-weight foams. The kickers I wear are heat-moulded into a shape that will gradually wear away but that won't fall apart like the old-fashioned ones used to.

One of my earlier mottos was to keep on improving and keep looking to see how I could maintain my edge over another player, and I think that this applies to the psychology of the game as well. The relationships within a team often depend on how well various individuals transmit their self-confidence, and in addition there is the other aspect of the 'you' versus 'them' situation. Whether it's a forward coming at you on a one-on-one basis, or a corner striker or a penalty stroke against you, psychology plays its part. At the 1978 World Cup I saved about 72% of the shots against me, and of the 12 penalty strokes I faced I saved eight. This sort of success, I believe, helps enormously because in the opposition's mind it builds up an image that you are difficult to beat, and they start formulating all sorts of negative thoughts before they've begun.

I can think of a couple of world class strikers that I've played against where it's been a marvellous case of psychological warfare! The German captain Heiner Dopp always likes to cut from left to right and then pulls the ball back in before shooting. I know he's scored a lot of goals like this because goalkeepers think he's going to continue across the circle and he just slips it in on the near post. By keeping my pad in the same position, I've learned to make him think that I've bought his dummy so that when he does roll the ball in I can effect a simple save.

The same sort of thing used to occur with Shahid of India who had an amazing dribble and he would always cause problems. He used come through on the open side (my right) and then he would neatly hit the ball reverse stick into the goal. And again I would fool him into thinking that I was beaten and rob him of the ball before he shot. The secret in these 'double bluff' situations is to convince the opposition that you have fallen for their feint.

Stefan Bloecher used to love to flick the ball into the goal at the end of a solo dribble. I knew that he would do this without fail, so I used to make him get to the end of his run a little sooner! I would go out to meet him but then stutter to make him think he'd beaten me. Then, while he prepared to flick, I would intercept to save it. Stefan did just that in the opening minute of the semi-final in Los Angeles and, after stuttering, I turned to make what appeared to be a spectacular diving save with my left hand in the corner of the goal. I was thrilled because as far as I was concerned I had made him shoot in that exact spot and I was prepared for the save.

It was more difficult when I didn't know players and then I had to create the double-bluff myself. I might stand to one side of the circle and give myself a little bit more room on my stick side and then force my opponent to shoot there, but of course I had the advantage of being able to bring my stick into action. Naturally, much depended on the experience of the attacking forward. The Korean forward, Man-Whe Kim, who scored the equaliser in our game against them in Seoul, sold me a superb dummy and then went round me like lightning to score. I was completely stranded.

The picture that says it all, with that gold medal grasped tightly in my hand. Was it worth those years of dedication? You bet!

A practice session three months before the Los Angeles Olympics. My equipment was shortly to develop into something rather more substantial (see below), but the style and skills remained largely the same.

One of those special moments – saving a penalty stroke against Ties Kruize of Holland, Los Angeles 1984. One of hockey's great ambassadors, Ties was the first to shake my hand at the end of the match.

My first World Cup, Buenos Aires 1978 – but what a distinguished line-up. From right to left: David Whitaker (GB Olympic coach), Bernard Cotton (then England captain), a young and reckless Paul Barber, the author (minus padding), Peter Frietag (coach to the Australia ladies gold medal-winning team at Seoul) and Norman Hughes (ex-captain of England and newly appointed England coach). All men who have served hockey with dedication for well over a decade!

The game which persuaded me not to retire! Our bronze medal-winning match against Australia in Los Angeles.

By the World Cup in 1986, Martyn Grimley, Paul Barber and I were the core of not only a successful penalty corner team but of the England and Great Britain defence. Three contrasting personalities, but united in the ultimate sporting objective – to be the best in the world.

The World Cup final against Australia, 1986. So near and yet so far: I knew that I had a lot of work to do if I was to leave the Olympics two years later with my ambition fulfilled.

My elder son, Simon. At 12 months he could dribble a hockey ball, and here – at 20 months – he is confident enough to take the World Cup field and show Dad how it should be done! I'm happy to boast that this boy has more sporting talents for his age that any other child I have seen, and as an ex-school teacher that has been many.

Oliver (left) and Simon share Dad's pride. I often wonder which sports they'll grow into and where their ambition will lie.

A proud moment – not the pride of achievement, but purely the honour of carrying the Union Jack for the world to see.

Colorsport

In the Olympic final, much depended on our ability to defend corners. The combined experience, skill and determination of Jon Potter, Richard Dodds, Paul Barber and myself proved a faultless team, defying the Germans at nine penalty corners.

Colorspe

Interviews! Even Steve Batchelor had a word or two after our final victory. Have you ever seen a happier bunch of lads?

Sean Kerly, Britain's prolific goalscorer, shares the final celebrations with me. For Sean the start of hopefully a long line of hockey victories; for me the conclusion of 12 years of international performance – the objective achieved!

Welcome home! The first chance to share my gold medal with Julie.

Reunited. After years of dedication to sport, time at last to devote myself full-time to my long-suffering family – who normally get just a quick 'thank you' and a pile of dirty washing for their pains!

Birmingham Post

Bromsgrove Advertiser

I don't really resort to gamesmanship on the whole, although I've had it used against me a lot of times! My old Australian adversary Terry Walsh delighted in calling me names – mostly 'pommie bashing' stuff and sometimes when they scored he'd come up to me and wag his finger in my face with a few choice expletives! A nice touch, though, was in the bronze medal play-off when we were giving our all against Australia. With the Aussies losing Walsh broke through and I went out to meet him with a sliding tackle (without my helmet on) and we collided. He accidentally hit me on the head and although he could still have played the ball he stopped to enquire: 'Are you alright mate?!'

Because of my added protection I was never bothered much by any attempts at rough play, but I did see plenty of it going on around me. One thing that does annoy me is the common ploy by forwards nowadays to pretend that they've been hit and put on great dramatic displays to win the umpire's sympathy. It's something I feel umpires should act on and put an immediate stop to. I seldom antagonise players deliberately, except probably my own team when I shout at them! Very occasionally I've signified my satisfaction by raising an arm in the air or by saying something like 'he's cracked lads' when a forward or corner striker keeps missing or shooting just past the post, but nothing more than that.

One of my most effective ways of improving was my use of what I call mental imagery. I would put myself in a specific situation and work out a set of reactions, and then set up that same situation in practice. I think you've got to do this in order to cope with a different set of circumstances and be able to react to something positively from memory, even if you haven't actually experienced it before. If you ever want to have a choice of responses then I think you have got to have tried each of those responses in a set position.

4
THE PRICE OF FAME

Early in my working career I was using teaching as my sponsor while I set out determinedly to achieve my ambitions as an international. I was quite lucky because that came about fairly quickly, and in my second year out of college I was a fully-fledged international in the England squad. It was no coincidence that around this time I met my wife, Julie, who was a very keen sports fan and an excellent tennis player. She fully understood the philosophies of how to win and why it was important to do so.

We had in fact originally met several years earlier at college and had got to know each other through mutual friends, but it was two Christmases after we'd left college that we met again and started going out. Both of were us pretty fiery characters at the time and the relationship was fairly stormy, although I think that was probably for the good because we were both looking for direction in our lives and were good sounding boards for one another. Julie is also from the Midlands and was brought up in Nuneaton, Warwickshire. As the relationship seemed to develop rather quickly into a serious one, we were faced with the problem of my sport and the restrictions it placed on us.

We couldn't do the sort of things that most young couples like to do and seldom went out for drinks or a meal which naturally placed stresses and strains on our relationship. Getting up early most mornings to train took its toll on me physically and so I quite often didn't want to go out anyway – I couldn't burn the candle at both ends. At that time Julie had taken a year off teaching and was working at Heathrow airport in an exciting and interesting job. The more serious the relationship became, the more we had to think about our future plans and whether or not we we were going to get married and where we were going to live. On our salaries it would have been impossible to find reasonable accommodation in the Kingston or Heathrow areas, and my hockey training was becoming very expensive. We were only given 3p a mile as a travelling allowance for international matches, and nothing at all for training. I was having to pay overnighting and travel costs and there was no kit allowance. There were added expenses that people don't often think about like the extra showers I would have to take, laundry bills and all the added match fee expenditure for the extra games I used to play. In those days I could easily spend all my budgeted monthly spending money on an item of expensive equipment. These financial demands, combined with my strict training regime, continued to put pressure on our relationship. I was forced to sell my car because I couldn't afford to run it any more, and inevitably I came in for a lot of criticism from people who didn't understand the situation. Soon it became a choice between hockey or . . . something.

Julie and I discussed everything and, although it's a cliché, it came down to 'marry me and my hockey!' and she realised that she couldn't fight it and finally accepted it. After that it was almost a complete turnabout and she became the driving force behind me, pushing me out the door to train and saying that we shouldn't go to the pub and that we should eat healthy foods. Breaking into the international scene came as quite a shock to Julie, because suddenly I was forced to spend such a lot of time away from her attending training weekends and playing in representative matches. She had always come to all the home matches, and now suddenly she was on her own for maybe one or two weeks at a time. It became lonely for her because she had lost touch with most of her old friends.

I found it was very difficult to get leave of absence from work. Being an international hockey player in those days meant absolutely nothing to most employers. I used to get permission to go away on condition that I took unpaid leave and that I paid the salary of the teacher who covered me. Any savings I had at the time would all be spent on paying someone to cover me. Luckily I had the fortune to meet a lady who was prepared to come in and do my teaching for me but because she didn't really need the money and was most sympathetic towards us, it cost me far less. I suppose you could say that she was my first sponsor because she actually took more financial burden off me in those days than anyone else.

In those days, expenses from the Hockey Association were virtually non-existant and what little we got hardly covered anything. No matter how hard we tried to improve this situation it was all to no avail. It was run by typical establishment-type characters who remembered the days of players and gentlemen and saw no reason to change. Hockey still had the 'public school' image and they figured (quite wrongly) that anyone who played hockey had the means to afford all the expenses.

There's a lovely little story about a famous member of the Hockey Association who has since retired but who typified the thinking of the day. I had sent in some expenses and was still waiting for the money owed to me and I spoke to him about it at an international function. He was most apologetic and suggested that I called in for it next time I was shopping. I explained to him that I lived in Kingston and that because I was working it would be rather difficult. In those days the offices were just around the corner from Harrods and he couldn't understand how I couldn't get in to collect the money because 'we're only a few minutes from Harrods!' I thought that summed up the situation perfectly because he honestly believed that all young men must shop at Harrods every week!

That sort of incident really used to annoy me and I was prepared to stand up against the system and fight it. When I did have the opportunity I did so, and although I was considered to be outspoken and damaging to the Association I believed it had to be done if the game was to progress. As far as I was concerned, the image of the game had to be changed, and to this day I'm glad that I stood my ground. There was a stage further on in my career when the Chairman of selectors asked me if I was considering retiring because it would probably be 'in my best interests'. I replied that if they could find someone who take over from me as the best goalkeeper in the world then I would be happy to step down! Until then they'd have to suffer me – and suffer me they did!

As we progressed towards the Moscow Olympics the manager, Roger Self, was still very unsure in his own mind how best to go about his tasks and he used us as guinea pigs. He gave us a very, very hard time with the onus on a strict physical regime, but without much direction. I found it gruelling and it really took its toll on my domestic life.

I would sometimes sit in the staff room and fall asleep in a chair. There would be horrified gasps from the other members of staff who thought I was mentally deranged, but actually I was completely exhausted. In fact what we were doing then would be hard to comprehend nowadays in view of the advances made in understanding the human body and training. I would start the day at about six o'clock in the morning with a three-mile run, then possibly interval training, and I'd finish that by doing a shuttle run with whoever it was I was training with. I pushed myself to such an extent that often I would be physically sick in the morning. I certainly don't get sick now because I have a better understanding of how to train, but it was my determination to fulfil the requirements – whatever they were – to make the team, that made me do it.

During lunch hour, I would go out and do another shuttle or a five-mile run in under thirty minutes. That may not be fantastic in itself, but it was the combined effects of daily training sessions and the lack of rest days that finally took its toll. In between my sleeps at breaktime I would hungrily devour a packet of biscuits and again there'd be startled looks from the staff! As an international team, it was no wonder that we never seemed to get any quicker on the runs because it was all too much, and it began to show in our games. We may have had the stamina but we lacked speed. Our performances were typical of a team of plodders because that was how we trained – no variety and no rest.

The most Julie saw of me at this time was the pile of dirty laundry in the bathroom. So with 1980 approaching and with all the sacrifices we had made, we decided to get married after the Olympics. We had made Moscow our goal, and our life's ambitions were set on my playing in them and so it was a terrible blow when someone else said we couldn't go. The marriage went ahead and the Olympics didn't. I think the marriage vows should have been changed to read 'in sickness and in health and in hockey!'

Financially we weren't terribly well-off, but we decided to take on a mortgage if we came across the right maisonette in the right area at the right time. We did just that but it was a derelict! Our two families were most supportive, although somewhat awe-struck at the sight of this falling-down three-storey maisonette! It was a beautiful old Victorian place in Caterham, Surrey but in desperate need of all sorts of work. My newly acquired father-in-law was horrified when we moved in on December 20th with only a couple of chests of drawers, a single mattress with no bottom to it, and some old curtains! There was no heating and no water and on December 21st I was flying off to Australia to play in a tournament.

My in-laws couldn't believe I was going to leave Julie even though the whole set-up didn't appear to concern either of us that much. They made last-minute arrangements for her to go and stay with some friends round the corner who had a convenient little granny flat that Julie could stay in. That winter was particularly harsh and I think one night the temperature dropped to minus 20 degrees, so it was definitely a sound decision for her to have moved out! On my return from an enjoyable tour in the Australian sunshine, the daily routine was about to change drastically.

In addition to my hockey and working commitments I now had to spend as much time as possible trying to renovate the house. Suddenly what I'd found difficult to squeeze into 18 hours I now had to squeeze in to 14 because I wanted to use the rest of the time working on our home. I rebuilt the chimney stack by climbing up using an old rope, because we couldn't afford to hire a roof ladder! I also used to go to the local wood and collect firewood because we couldn't afford to buy it. It sounds a bit dramatic, but it was a hard and tight situation because in no way did we ever restrict ourselves on the commitment to hockey.

We suffered a lot of criticism once again from people who didn't appreciate our priorities, and who felt it was far more important to get things like curtain rails up and buy coal for the house instead of a new pair of goalkeeping pads. Julie had to resist the temptation of asking me to work constantly on the house and it inevitably put a strain on her. For my part I became even more determined to succeed with my hockey goal because I could appreciate all that Julie was giving up and how difficult things were. I would say that it was an experience that most couples should go through because, despite the hardships, we had loads of fun working together on the house and slowly but surely we were able to recognize the value of what we'd achieved. It didn't all go smoothly, however; I remember an amusing incident when I had just put all the floorboards down upstairs and put in a new ceiling on the room below, and Julie brought me a cup of coffee. She immediately fell straight through the boards, through the ceiling and ten foot down to the floor below. Luckily she wasn't hurt apart from a sore backside and we laughed ourselves silly over it!

Setting aside the time to do all this DIY wasn't easy, and I found it almost impossible ever to find a full day. Being a schoolteacher was certainly convenient because I could always make use of the holidays and I would carefully plan my days. Perhaps I would train in the morning, work on the house all afternoon and then at tea time I might have to go to Crystal Palace or whatever. But during term time it was even harder to squeeze everything in. Sometimes I would start on a room at eight o'clock at night after getting in from a tiring training session. I'd be eating as I was painting and sometimes work through until five the next morning to get it finished. I found I came to the stage where it was a case of 'do I or don't I get up for a run at six a.m?', and when I missed going I would have such a guilty conscience by lunchtime that I would push myself even harder the next time. In retrospect, though, it would have been far more beneficial if I hadn't been so stupid and realised I couldn't run myself in to the ground.

We carried on in our house, and the political wranglings over who did or didn't go to the 1984 Los Angeles Olympics continued. The players had little say in all these matters, and most went along quite happily with what was being decided. With all this petty politics, however, I saw the fulfilment of my ambition drifting away from me again. Rather than remaining silent I became an antagonist, and came in strongly to support any suggestion that might help Britain qualify for the Olympics. I became more and more outspoken and was often considered the voice of the team. Many of the people who were causing my selfish fear had no idea what playing in the Games meant to me and how difficult it was for me to accept failure.

At last Julie and I finished our house and we agreed to have a huge dinner to celebrate. We invited all our friends who had generously given us meals when the cooker still wasn't installed or the gas wasn't on and when things were generally chaotic. The house was looking gorgeous, it had real character and Julie had done a wonderful job designing half-timbered walls, beautiful cornices and an old open fireplace. The dining room was the last room to be completed and I had laid the carpet the night before. We had a memorable evening and drank a few bottles of wine and then Julie said that she had an important announcement to make! We all held our breath as she boldly told everyone there: 'We're moving!'

Her reasoning was that the house wasn't big enough for the family which we eventually wanted to have, and now that it was finished we could sell it. Although it made sense at the time because of the state of the property market, and we knew it would be a good time to move, it certainly came as a shock to the system! Julie and I had discussed at length the subject of having children – when would be best time to start a family, how old Julie wanted to be and so on. I felt that it would be extremely unfair on Julie and any children that we might have if I was commited the way I was to hockey, and that it would be best for all of us to put off starting a family until I had achieved what I had set out to do.

The build-up to the 1984 Olympics was now beginning. From the players' point of view, it all boiled down to the tournament in Hong Kong, where we thought that finishing in the first three would be good enough to guarantee Britain's place. Unfortunately it didn't turn out quite like that, and we came fourth. After a very long meeting, the FIH invited Malaysia to Los Angeles. I believed that we had done enough to secure a place in the Olympics, especially since we had finished ahead of Malaysia. However, our system hadn't been particularly successful, we didn't play to our full potential and we were disorganised and badly managed. Great Britain were named as first reserves.

This was tantamount to the destruction of my international career, but I was prepared to battle on. Having got over the initial disappointment, I found my best form and turned in good club performances for East Grinstead where we won everything from the league to the national cup. I managed to put the Olympics to the back of my mind. With so much more time on my hands, a bigger house and my international career as good as finished, we decided to start a family in 1984. I didn't consider 1988 at any stage, and as far as I was concerned at that time, my Olympic ambition would remain unfulfilled.

It was a difficult decision to have children and probably the most argumentative time of our whole relationship. We often thought of the times when I had turned down jobs offered to me on condition that I gave up hockey. That was always very disappointing and yet another example of just how much I had been prepared to sacrifice in order to get to the Games. Things had changed for the better in 1982, when I met someone who was influential enough in the educational world to ensure that I was given an additional 21 days absence a year *with* pay. What a cause for celebration that was! I became quite despondent about my chances of promotion, however, as it became painfully obvious that Ian Taylor and his hockey were not compatible in a teaching situation.

The great turnabout occurred at the end of 1983, when I was offered a job at Stoke Brunswick School in Ashurstwood, near East Grinstead. The Headmaster, Mark Ellerton, was a great sports fan and understood everything that I spoke about. He was not only co-operative with my sport but he enjoyed it, talked about it and was quite happy to pay me when I had to go away. He deemed it a great honour to be chosen to represent one's country. At last I had actually found an employer who was willing to support me – even though it was a rather ironic situation since I intended to retire before too long. I kept up a general level of training and began enjoying life a lot more. Julie fell pregnant, we bought a dog and I was ready to settle down into normal family life.

Julie was about three or four months pregnant when she 'phoned me one day at school. I couldn't work out what she was saying at all because she was screaming and shouting down the 'phone, and I got into quite a panic. Eventually I managed to understand that I should go and put on the TV or the radio because the Russians had withdrawn from the Olympics. Up until this stage I had never considered that a nation might refuse to go, and I couldn't contemplate getting to the Olympics by default. I was completely taken aback by the news. Part of me wanted to jump for joy and celebrate, but the rest of me wanted to be with Julie during her pregnancy.

I was also extremely annoyed that I had lost all those months of training time.

It was strange doing interviews at that time, because the press would ask me how I was expecting to do and I would reply that I intended to win a gold medal. They found it impossible to take me seriously! They considered that we were thirteenth and didn't stand a chance of succeeding, and they couldn't relate to the numerous situations that I'd been in over the years where we had played in tournaments and only missed out on the final place or a medal by the odd goal. We had toured Australia and beaten them and I was confident that we could put it together and do well in Los Angeles. I think that was my most trying period with the media.

We weren't the best team in the world by a long way, but I knew we were capable of taking on the world's best and I believed that in the right circumstances, in the right draw, we could go out and win the gold. I can understand people having reservations, though, since we had never beaten Pakistan before, although we went on to draw with them in Los Angeles and beat them in Saudia Arabia the following January.

My intensified training programme tore me away from being the caring, helpful husband Julie needed. I became preoccupied with my own selfish requirements – what I needed to get me into the best condition, where I needed to go and train, where I should go to practise, which games I should play on what weekend and where. The programme that we were required to keep to for 12 weeks before the Games meant something like three days in five away from the house. If I wasn't on long training weekends or short tours to Europe I would be coming in after midnight from Crystal Palace when Julie was fast asleep, and up again for a run at six the next morning. There would just be the passing kiss at breakfast, how are you and where are you tonight?!

There was conflict between us and we had the added problem of the financial implications, but it's an indication the complete dedication in both of our lives that we didn't even consider the monetary side. All the driving and petrol came to huge amounts, and I remember paying out half my salary one month on petrol bills. I think in that year I did about 22,000 miles – virtually all for hockey, since I cycled to work. My headmaster kept his word and was a source of enormous encouragement to us both.

I found that I was able to motivate myself, but I also gained inspiration from Roger Self, who had been appointed as our manager, and who had a tremendous desire for the team to succeed. He realised that we were lagging behind in our physical work and insisted on pushing us to extremes. This time around, however, I was far more sensible in training and varied it much more by combining my hockey training with swimming and a bit of squash. Because there were only about three suitable artificial hockey surfaces in the country at the time, I was forever having to think about where I could train and what would be convenient times. It was impossible to book time as an individual at Crystal Palace and the closest one was in Crawley. I 'phoned up to book it, but it was out of the question because of the local pubs' football league. Sean Kerly, Steve Batchelor, Richard Leman and myself went along nevertheless, and could be seen practising for the Olympics on the five yards behind the goal! We didn't consider what a ludicrous situation we were in at the time, because we were just happy to have the chance to go to Los Angeles. We knew that we had to prepare as best we could.

Arriving in Los Angeles was an eye-opener for all for us. No one asked us for overnighting fees and we didn't have to think about where we were going to find the money to pay for the tournament. We were actually given kit and nobody asked us for £15 towards it! The Olympic Games was already living up to its reputation. The British Olympic Association paid us some expenses and we were astounded at the gesture. However, the team's joy was short lived. They were asked to pay most of the expenses back to the management to help pay for the specialised goalkeeping equipment that Veryan and I needed to buy to protect us when we used the horizontal style of 'keeping that Roger Self insisted on. We were not very popular!

When I returned with the bronze, I was filled with the excitement of the Olympic Games and I was confident that we had the potential to go on to greater things in 1988. I desperately wanted to be a part of that, and it was then that the enormity of Julie's sacrifices struck me. She had been so confident that I would retire and had given up all hopes of my gold medal, we had planned our life accordingly, and all of a sudden life had taken a completely different direction. I had come home in August, Simon was due at the end of October and Julie was now faced with the prospect of four more years of me being involved in a hectic schedule. There were lots of arguments and long discussions and in the end Julie agreed that I could continue to achieve my ambition. I don't think she'd ever admit it but one of the deciding factors, I'm sure, was that she didn't want me to be an 'if only', always bemoaning what might have been. If I had retired from international competition at that stage then she knew I would have been unbearable in years to come.

The public reaction to our bronze medal was overwhelming and naturally there was massive media interest. I was asked to appear on television programmes such as 'Wogan', 'Question of Sport' and 'Sports Team of the Year', all of which was most enjoyable and something I hadn't experienced before, but was also very time-consuming. I was already working a six day week as a schoolteacher and was expected to put in long hours. The extra engagements and my hockey training placed a big burden on Julie who was constantly answering the 'phone and being asked to arrange my diary for me. All the invitations to sporting and community events, the lavish dinners and gifts were lovely – but where was Julie? I could be at the Hilton for my meal but poor Julie would have to cook for herself at home. We lived a long way from both of our parents which made it even more difficult for her because she could never just pop in to see them. Julie was stuck at home, whilst I selfishly continued with sport and career and lapped up the media attention, with a few weeks left before the birth of our first child. We did once go to a ball together, however, and she's probably one of the few women who've gone to a ball eight months, three weeks and four days pregnant! We took the precaution of asking Richard Dodds (who is a doctor) to sit close to us just in case, but happily nothing happened!

When Simon was born the strain of my 'double life' became even more painful, and I found I was pitting my hockey against much more than Julie. It wasn't made any better when the team was invited to play in so many more hockey tournaments. Simon was only eight days old when I had to go to Karachi to the Champions' trophy. Julie was once again all alone.

I know it was selfish but I was unrepentant about going off, and although I felt pangs of guilt I also knew that this was what I had to do. The guilt was suppressed by my ambition. I had hardly arrived home from Karachi when I informed Julie that on New Year's day I would be off to the United Arab Emirates to another tournament for about a week. It was another good opportunity because the trip would pay for a lot of future training expenses, and that was most unusual. We had had numerous fund-raising activities in the past and on one occasion we had run from Liverpool to London to finance a tour to Australia, so when you consider that sort of effort, a free trip was too good to miss. Again Julie was left at home while I played in the sunshine.

In October the following year there was another Champions' trophy, but this time it was in Australia and Julie announced that if I wanted to go then she would accompany me. That was the first time she had ever been to a tournament and she picked the one that was furthest away and the most expensive. We scraped the money together and she stayed with friends in Perth. The management couldn't comprehend women being involved in hockey and I think the most we saw of each other was after the game for an hour or so on about three occasions. We ended up spending a lot of money for her to have a holiday by herself when she could have gone somewhere else and probably had a much better time – but at least it showed her what the life of an international hockey player was all about.

Touring abroad is certainly not as glamorous as everyone supposes. I've been to Australia at least eight times and yet I couldn't tell you much more about the country than anyone who has watched a documentary programme on it. I've seen the airports, hotels, playing fields and coach rides in between. I was lucky enough once to be on a coach in Canberra when a kangaroo appeared but that's the only time I've ever seen one. I'm familiar with cuisines around the world and I know a bit about the people in various countries but not much more.

When I add it up I've been to Pakistan about twenty times and India two or three, as well as Australia, Mexico, Argentina, Brazil, USA, Moscow, Malaysia, Singapore and Hong Kong. I've been to the major European cities countless times. If I had actually saved all the money that I've spent on hockey and gone on normal holidays to all those countries I would have had a marvellous life. But of course there have been great moments and I know, for example, that without my hockey I would never have been able to play a round of golf at the Royal Hong Kong – which was a real treat and something I could never have afforded otherwise. The worst thing is not being able to have shared it all with my family.

Hockey's image went from strength to strength after Los Angeles, and I continued to play in tournaments preparing for the World Cup in London. The pressure was that I had a family, mortgage commitments, and a job which all made demands on me. Mark Ellerton, my headmster, kept his word and remained a constant source of support. I felt that the World Cup in Willesden in 1986 would be an ideal opportunity to say 'thank you' to all those people like Julie and my parents who had faithfully stood by me over the years, and another friend called Derek Baden who had encouraged and helped me overcome difficult obstacles and periods in my career.

The World Cup provided a chance to perform, a stage within my home country for everyone to come and experience all the excitement of a tournament. In an egotistical way I wanted to go out and show all these people that I was the best in the world, because we had never really played many internationals in England. I am disappointed that when I was called on to represent England in England, I had to do so as part of a Lions team and therefore was not eligible for a cap. Similarly, when Australia or Pakistan toured England we tended to form occasional sides such as English X1 or the President's X1, whilst the team playing against us treated it as a full international and were awarded caps. I know that to this day I've got 20-odd more caps than those accredited to me. I retired on 174 caps but I've played in approximately 196 internationals.

England received an enormous amount of media attention at the World Cup, and although I never really felt under much pressure I was aware of it. On the domestic scene, Julie and I had decided to carry on as though I had retired for the sake of the family and, with our usual sense of impeccable timing, Oliver was due to the end of the World Cup! So it was Julie who was once again under pressure – as I happily went on with my preparations and she was forced to stay at home and look after Simon, aged 18 months. That's why I've so often made a big thing about thanking her, because most people have simply no idea what she's been through. Throughout our married life Julie has willingly dealt with all the press enquiries, invitations and arrangements for our various engagements. It wasn't difficult, though, for her to get a firm commitment from me that I would retire after the 1988 Olympics, whatever the outcome. I wanted to retire at the top, and although there are stages of the top, my 'top' was to be in the best team and win the gold medal.

The run-up to Seoul put a great stress on both of us. I was haunted by nagging doubts – whether Great Britain wouldn't qualify on goal difference, or what if I had a shocking tournament or we lost in the final. I think that this obsessive worry affected our lives. Julie has subsequently told me how strained I looked at the time and how short tempered I was before I left. The physical effects of tiredness, long drives and training all took their toll. But she has also said that as I stood on the rostrum she could almost see the strain draining from me, and an hour later when we spoke by satellite I was almost back to my old self.

We were well aware of the fact that our two sons rarely saw their grandparents and so, after discussing it with one another, we decided to move back to the Midlands because there was no chance of our parents making the move to the south-east. It was always such a long way to drive if we wanted to see them, and driving was often the last thing I felt like doing. The wheels were set in motion, and in the few months preceding Seoul we were making good progress. We had found a house and, as usual, I was preparing for yet another tournament and was off to Lahore. Contracts for the house still hadn't been exchanged and I remember phoning up from Pakistan to see whether the money had been paid over. All I had managed to do in the house in the two days I was there before leaving for the tournament was put up the bunk beds in the boys' room! One of the worst things about leaving East Grinstead was moving away from the many friends we had made there. I found it very painful.

In the couple of years prior to Seoul it was noticeable how much more financial assistance became available. For example I was asked to design goalkeeping equipment for Slazenger and for the first time I wasn't having to scrounge around for it and write off to manufacturers pleading for trade prices. This was unprecedented! The Sports Aid Foundation also helped with sizeable amounts to offset expenses, and for the first time ever we didn't have to pay for any overnighting at the World Cup. So little by little the scene was improving and our success was reaping welcome financial rewards.

The hobby I had so actively pursued was costing me less and less – with the expenses of a family man the handouts were most welcome. I'm not sure that I shall be a teacher for life, and I'm not convinced that I would have become one had I not nurtured this Olympic ambition. Perhaps I would have been tempted to enter into professional cricket, but I could never have won Olympic gold if I had. I don't resent Peter Shilton earning as much as he does for being a soccer goalkeeper, because the hockey choice was always mine and both Julie and I knew what the personal and financial cost of the Olympic dream would be.

I missed seeing my children grow up and there are great chunks of their lives, particularly when they were babies, that passed me by. To go away and leave your one-week-old son and see him four weeks later means missing big part of his life, and I wanted to see his first giggle, the first time he reacted to movement or the first time he looked me in the eyes. It really is extremely difficult to quantify what hockey has cost me in family terms and I certainly haven't benefited in monetary terms.

The interest in hockey has certainly expanded when I compare it to the aftermath of Los Angeles. Julie is now able to accompany me to many of the functions because it's is so much easier to get babysitters and I'm much happier about that. The male bias on all the invitations I've received is astonishing, however. We were invited to a civic reception when I got back from Seoul, and when we arrived at the door the organizers requested that Julie sit at another table and not with me. I was most annoyed and said that if they wanted to celebrate the gold medal, which in my opinion was 'our' gold medal not 'mine', then we would either have to sit together or leave. Thankfully, it was all resolved amicably.

Julie has had the chore of sorting out all my invitations, but the bulk of them exclude her. It really is quite unbelievable and a fine example of how people forget Julie's immeasurable part in my triumph. It has to be a special occasion for me to accept without her. An evening with Julie means a lot to me now, especially after all the ones I've had without her, so whenever possible she accompanies me.

5
HOCKEY HYPOCRISY: MY LIFE AS A DISSIDENT

I think that one of the most common adjectives used to describe me in the hockey world has been 'cynical'. I think that that's a trait that has developed with due cause. I am a cynic and I am a critical person, but right from an early age I've been like that and I've always done it to be positive. Whether I've criticised religion, politics, standards or behaviour, I've always done so because I've been looking for an answer. And I think criticism breeds cynicism.

I believe very strongly that if you're going to be critical then you've got to be prepared to stand up to what you've said. But because of the strength of some of my convictions, I admit that I have been particularly forthright in the past. Some people may have construed what I've said as abusive, but whatever I've said has been as a result of ardent belief and complete honesty. If I've been wrong, then it's been an honest mistake.

I'm a very logical person and there's always a definite sequence to my actions and certainly to my thoughts. So if I've voiced an opinion, that opinion has always been the result of a sequence of events and I would have researched the background to the issue as much as possible beforehand. When I was younger I would fly off the handle much quicker, but my words are weighed up extremely carefully nowadays. When people wonder if I realise the consequences of what I'm saying, the answer is 'of course,' and I've measured that before I've actually said it. I only ever said things about hockey in the hope that in the long run the game would benefit.

I am a very strong-willed character, and I'm sure I always have been. I have tried very hard in recent years to be as objective as possible and I've deliberately examined the other side of the coin before presenting my argument. I find criticism hard to accept if it's negative, but like most people I'm always willing to listen if it's constructive.

I first came across hypocrisy in hockey when I became a regular member in the senior international side. Before that I had little idea of what went on behind the scenes and from schoolboy level through the junior ranks I would arrive at a game, pay my match fee, play, shower and go home. But when the sanctimoniousness of officialdom affected someone I loved my response was quick and angry. I remember once arriving at a ground in Bishop's Stortford to play for England, with Julie in the car with me who was going to watch the match. It wasn't my first international but it was definitely one of the earlier ones at home. We had made sure we got there just before lunch so that we had could have a light snack before the game. When we arrived at the gate a Hockey Association official stopped me and after acknowledging who I was, he said that Julie would have to pay. I felt that very hard to accept and it made me exceedingly angry. That small incident brought home to me the extent of hypocrisy that existed in hockey and reinforced what I had already observed on several tours abroad.

The chef de missions always seemed to enjoy the comforts of first class travel when we went on overseas tours, while the rest of us sat in economy. It was only at the time of the incident at the gate that I began to wonder who was actually paying for all these trips. After I'd parted with my £3 or so for Julie, who was then my fiancée, I watched all the hockey officials come rolling in and go to their exclusive lounge. The players weren't allowed in to enjoy the free bar and comfort of the room, and the general public certainly weren't.

I paid attention to all this, and I reflected that of course there has to be a certain amount of promotion and support of the companies that had put money into the game, but who was actually footing the bill? Where was my overnighting money going, did those officials pay their £3 entrance money and are any of them going to get outside to actually watch the game? Are they ensconced in the bar all afternoon? As a young man who wanted to get things done it wasn't hard for me to set on a road to try and put it right, and if I had to step on toes in the process, I was perfectly prepared to do so. Obviously I was rather immature at the time but I was also impatient to get the game moving forward – and impatient for my own success – but what wore me down more than anything was the system operating at the time. I had become an unwilling pawn in the system and and I believed I could do something about it. Whether or not I actually voiced my discontent was a decision I had to make.

The major problem as I saw it was the personnel involved in the game. They were long-standing voluntary members who had given up a lot of their time, without pay, to develop an organisation that suited them perfectly. The game was barely ticking over, the same old schools were playing hockey, England and British teams were still considered 'awfully nice' to invite to tournaments, although they would never win much. So naturally they weren't terribly pleased when I started to request a few changes and asked that players' wives could attend matches without having to pay, and pointed out that it might be nice if the opposition were treated to a drink after the game and not just the opposition's officials.

The people replacing those at the top were in the same mould as those retiring. It was the same all the way through the country and regional organisation, with privately-sponsored men setting themselves up in influential positions. The whole process was self-perpetuating which aggravated me intensely. I was reminded of it every time I went away on tour because there were constantly members of the Association going along for the 'jolly'. Our opponents always seemed to have a far more professional attitude. I'll never forget someone called Keith Merton from the Australian board who was responsible for the development of their game. It was staggering to be able to watch him actually working hard – he not only performed his duties as a diplomat but he seemed to make an incredible number of business contacts as well. When you see chaps like that then you automatically compare them with people in a similar situation over here. I don't disagree with the principle of someone from the Association acting as a representative, but just as the team, coach and manager earn their positions, then so should anyone else. All the trip appeared to be in those days was a lot of gin and tonics, first-class food and luxurious travel and hotels.

I was playing for Slough hockey club at about this time and we were a very successful side. We had practically the whole Buckinghamshire team and we won the nationals, London league, county championships, and we were generally involved in anything that was considered prestigious in club hockey. But it never failed to amaze me when the same sort of people turned up at every match. It was difficult to see their actual purpose and when I read names of people who were supposed to be organisers of tournaments I couldn't believe it because they never seemed to do a thing. However, they were always there, staying in the best hotels and travelling first class.

One incident I clearly recall was when I was selected for a Hockey Association X1 to play in an afternoon game. It must have been fairly early on in my career for me to have had the time to play in it. At the station I met the then secretary general on the HA, Colonel Dennis Eagan, who was the only full-time paid employee of the Association (apart from secretaries). We had a chat on the platform and he was very pleasant while we waited to catch the train to Oxford. I stood there, kitbag in hand, and then the train pulled in. Dennis jumped in to the first available carriage, first class of course, and as I was about to follow him he asked:

'Have you got a first class ticket?'

'No,' I replied.

'Well I have,' he said. 'The ticket inspector won't let you stay in here.' And off I trundled to a second class compartment after being informed in a less than subtle way that he didn't want to travel with me! He was most polite at the other end and we resumed our conversation but I thought what an awful distinction it was and that I, as a player, had to pay for most of the journey out of my own pocket.

It became a general talking point and numerous players at all levels began to voice their dissatisfaction. The system didn't change until the appointment of Phil Appleyard as President a few years ago.

The more involved I became in my own game the less time I had to pursue the issue, but what really set me going again was the government's boycott of the 1980 Moscow Olmpics and the HA's handling of the whole affair. We had qualified for the Games and although an Olympic 16 hadn't yet been picked I felt that I was playing well enough to merit selection. In fact the squad was going to be announced about two weeks after we actually heard that Britain had boycotted. I take an interest in current affairs and when I heard about the Russian invasion of Afghanistan I immediately became concerned, although it never crossed my mind that it might affect me personally in any way.

It was only the next day that I heard that the British government had condemned the invasion and were calling on counter measures from other countries. Later that day I heard that Mrs Thatcher had asked for participating members and associate members of the British Olympic Association to boycott the Games as a protest. When I heard this I didn't think that the majority of people would go ahead with it, because I thought that most personal and national objectives would be greater than the act of pulling out of an Olympic Games.

I received an anonymous phonecall a couple of days later telling me that the GB Board, made up of the four constituent countries, had convened an emergency meeting and had decided to boycott. Apparently the meeting had voted four to one in favour of the boycott, and it is rumoured that England had put forward a very strong case which swayed the others. Immediately every possible emotion ranging from anger to frustration erupted. I had lived for the Games for years and now, after working so hard to secure my place, someone else had told me I wasn't going without even asking me. I was outraged.

There had been no voting, no discussion and a decision had been reached by a few men who considered it their absolute right to come to the judgemement. Whether the decision to boycott was right or wrong was quite immaterial. What was wrong was that the players were totally excluded. It didn't take long for the press to realise that I was very happy to speak my mind and I became embroiled in all sorts of arguments and programmes. The controversy seemed to interest the news pages and programmes as well as the sports side, and within a short space of time the HA reluctantly called a general meeting for representatives from all the Associations. It was probably the quickest the HA had moved in years!

All the protests, or at least the majority, had come from England and it was felt, therefore, that a constitutional meeting concerning the procedures should be held. The meeting was scheduled to take place in a hotel in Birmingham, presumably because the city was fairly central and easily reached. But those with a more devious mind believed that because the vast majority of the antagonism had come from the south-east, a meeting had conveniently been called in Birmingham for the first time ever. After that, meetings continued to be held in London. It was also coincidental that several crucial matches scheduled for that day weren't allowed to be postponed.

I had received considerable backing for my stand on the issue, some of it quite open and some quietly whispered to me, but there was also a lot 'gentle advice' given to me and of course I suffered scathing personal attacks from some quarters. I even had the animal rights organisations writing to me and asking me if I knew what the Soviet tanks were doing to the animals as they advanced along roads! They failed to see that it wasn't the question of the boycott that concerned me, but the principle behind how the decision was reached.

I was warned off by several members of the HA, and it was interesting that they happened to be the same people whom I had crossed in my earlier battle against the free gin and tonic brigade. Notice of the meeting had been sent to all the associate members of the HA. It was a post-lunch affair and I was accompanied by Julie and my parents, all of whom were anxious to be present. We arrived at about lunchtime – no way was I going to be late! The first thing I noticed as I went past the restaurant was a large contingent of HA officials sitting down and enjoying a delicious dinner! Even some men I considered to be on the 'right' side of hockey were in there, and although several claimed to have paid for their own meals it still rankled me that such hypocrisy was being flaunted on such a sensitive occasion. As I recall I had a packet of crisps for my lunch!

It wasn't too long before we made our way to the door where the meeting was to be held and were immediately confronted with a problem. In a new and secret policy, hitherto totally unannounced by the HA, it was revealed that only one member per club could attend as a spectator. People were being scrutinised and rejected at the door. Naturally I was furious, and instantly we made my parents and Julie members of all sorts of clubs which wasn't awfully honest but they were determined to be there.

Once inside the meeting, which was to be overseen by a special executive committee, I was amazed to observe that it was to be chaired by a Major General Sir Gerald Duke. I had never seen nor heard of the gentleman in my entire life, and in the nine years since that day I have never seen nor heard of him again! To my knowledge he had never been to a hockey match I had ever played in and I certainly had never seen him at an international. Not only that but there were all sorts of other life vice-presidents present, some of whom literally had to be wheeled in. I harboured the suspicion that perhaps this meeting was going to be stage-managed! A large number of the counties sent representatives and the meeting was run fairly, with most people being given a say, although I did think that some speeches were directed and manipulated. It's certainly not easy to swing opinion at a large meeting, and a lot of the issues were soon lost. I think there were only about three members of the squad there, but we were given the chance to have our say. I suppose our motives were selfish, but we did feel that since the British Olympic Association wasn't stopping athletes from taking part, then why should the HA stop us?

I think that it was grossly unfair to involve all the vice-presidents and I don't think we ever had a chance of changing anything, but because the meeting was run constitutionally and fairly I had to accept the consequences. At the end of the meeting it was only a marginal vote that upheld the original decision. The wind was completely taken out of my sails and I must admit that I felt completely demoralised when I left. I don't even remember leaving the room or getting back to Kingston.

In retrospect it's difficult to say exactly why the vote went the way it did, but after the affair at least two officials involved in the hockey organisation got promotion within the government. I really do believe that there were a lot of people, for a variety of reasons, who accepted Mrs Thatcher's recommendation without even thinking about it from hockey's viewpoint. I followed up the whole affair with regional TV and radio interviews, but it wasn't regarded as all that newsworthy by a lot of the press. I thought I had done a reasonable amount of good by shouting loudly and making myself heard, but ultimately I was no more than an irritable little thorn in the side of an old establishment that had won it's way.

In the aftermath of all my protests, it was interesting that if ever there was a letter going out inviting players to a training weekend, mine never quite arrived until after it had taken place. My personal contacts within the game kept me well informed, however, and I never actually missed one. There were also questions asked about some of my expense claims and things like why was I claiming £11.50 and not £10.29 were often the bone of contention. Whether or not it would have been a problem if I had kept quiet about Moscow is open to opinion.

There were other niggling incidents but I tried not to let them get to me and I continued normally in the hope that perhaps I was doing some good. Some people suggested that all the publicity was bad for the game but even in hindsight I don't feel I should have kept quiet. I don't think I did any harm – what harm could I do? The game was in the pits with regard to administration, results and image, and simply couldn't sink any further.

In September 1980 I played a game for England against Zimbabwe in Norwich. The match ended in an uninspiring 1–1 draw and I hardly touched the ball but there was an interesting incident after the match. There was quite a good sized crowd and a marquee had been erected where we had a sandwich afterwards before going on to a club house in the area. Whilst we were sitting upstairs in the bar the chairman of selectors, Clive Chapman, came over to me and said: 'Well Ian, when are you thinking of retiring?' During the conversation I had with him he inferred that GB wouldn't qualify for the next Olympics and that there wasn't really much of a future for me in the game. It didn't take me long to inform him that I had no intention of retiring but would happily do so when they found someone better!

Although I should have been wiser by this stage, I found that I became even more rebellious particularly on the domestic scene. I drove my car through a barrier once at a London league final when they insisted that Julie paid. I think I even took the attendant with it on the bonnet of the car! I certainly didn't intend to hurt anybody but my feelings were that strong. Likewise, if there was a patrons only bar at an international with officials inside enjoying themselves, not really promoting the game but just in a different venue for their latest cocktail party, I would be incensed. It was a naive attitude but I would storm in and gatecrash. In fact very often I would be raging in to snatch a free orange juice! Again it was the principle of the matter and I only did it because I thought that these sort of people should be beaten.

I had tried to be positive by making various proposals. For example I suggested that we should invite more international teams over to play in England. I remember once having a discussion with an official who was heavily involved in the promotion of the game, and Phil Appleyard, who was responsible for the organisation of the World Cup. This official received my suggestion about teams touring England, and gave me a whole host of reasons as to why it wasn't possible. His closing statement, which effectively sealed his fate, was 'who on earth would want to sponsor hockey – there is nothing to sponsor.'

The problem was was that this man was one of the chief figures in promoting hockey in England and, by virtue of his seniority, was almost certainly going to be voted onto Phil Appleyard's World Cup committee. It came as no surprise when Phil excluded him. Unfortunately the opinion he expressed was typical of many officials at the time. We still had to pay our travel, overnighting and tickets and although we had been filling in Sports Aid foundation forms since 1978, we never saw any of the money which was paid out. As a result of an article that appeared concerning my financial plight I was informed by the SAF that they had been paying out to Ian Taylor since 1978. Needless to say I hadn't received any of it, and their reply was that the money had been given to the HA and if I hadn't received it I should have complained. What they didn't realise was that the system didn't allow us to complain. Whatever arguments we had could be thrown straight back at us because of the lack of sponsorship and the fact that the money was being used for training weekends. It was a vicious circle: we couldn't develop the game because of the people that were running it and the game wouldn't develop until the personnel changed.

Things quietened down a bit, Ian Taylor probably matured and by the beginning of 1984 I had tired fighting the establishment. I lost interest in most of the national domestic tournaments because I didn't believe in what they stood for. I made no positive contribution to the administration or organisation of the game although I was very enthusiastic about coaching youngsters. I must admit though that whenever an opinion was sought on hockey I seemed to be the one the press interviewed. I felt I was experienced enough to make sure that what I wanted would appear in the article rather than what the author wanted to portray.

The media hype that followed the British success in Los Angeles meant a difficult time for me. I had to be very careful about what I said because people kept telling me that negative contributions would do the hockey cause no good at all. People were still wary of what I was doing, even though I was making a conscious effort not to contradict what the HA was saying to potential sponsors and others.

The changes that eventually took place were slow and cumbersome and often for the wrong reasons. I think some men were frightened of the amount of work that would be required if they capitalised on the 1984 result, and realised that their decisions would then be scrutinised. Life in the goldfish bowl, watched closely by the Sports Council, the Sports Minister and various sporting bodies, might not be very pleasant! What the officials were doing was neither quick enough nor good enough. The appointment of regional development officers should have taken place almost immediately after we won the bronze to get the maximum mileage out of it, not six or eight months away as was happening.

I think that this situation has changed for the better now and there is far more enthusiasm and advance planning. There are still faults, for example, why are regional development officers only part-time? Clubs are crying out for professional advice and are often swamped on a Sunday morning when up to a hundred children turn up to play. I still think more dynamism is necessary, and we should have a sales and marketing network that would be unsurpassed when it came to supplying anything to do with hockey. I'm confident that the financial support could be obtained to implement these ideas, but we need to act far more swiftly than we are at the moment.

I think that if we don't take a gamble now, after countless meetings and feasibility reports, we can never expect to maximise on the current wave of enthusiasm. International tournaments staged in England should be another priority. My criticism only stems from a deep desire to see the best done for a sport I love.

When the World Cup was held in London in 1986 it was also the centenary of the Hockey Association. It was to be the showpiece of our country and there were extravagant dinners and functions to honour the occasion. There was just one problem. The England team manager informed us that we wouldn't be having smart new blazers like all the officials but that we were to wear the blazers from the 1985 tour of Australia. All we had to do was change the badge. I thought it was disgraceful – we would have to attend social events at number ten Downing Street and in the City in a jumble of blazers and with odd badges sewn on. I spoke to the president, Phil Appleyard, and within hours rather than days he had arranged blazers for us. It was quite amusing because when any of us had mentioned it previously to other officials, we had been given a multitude of excuses as to why we couldn't be smartly turned out.

The appointment of Phil Appleyard as the President of the HA in 1985 was inspired, and without doubt he has done more to advance the cause of hockey that most of his predecessors. Even so I, remember at the World Cup in 1986 and unsavoury incident regarding Julie when she came along to watch one of the days when we were approaching the semi-finals. She is obviously well known to many of the officials, but when she arrived she discovered that she had been given a ticket for the standing-only area, on the far side of the ground. Julie was informed that it was impossible for her to sit in the officials stand which was by no means full and a certain hockey official, who was well acquainted with her, refused to allow her to sit in the reserved area and insisted she make her way over to the far side. Julie was eight and a half months pregnant at the time. It was only when she met Roger Dakin, the Public Relations Director, on her way round that he insisted she sit in the official enclosure.

It's occurrences such as this which begin to break down the relationship between players and officials. I have lots of friends in the cricket world and I know that it would be unheard of for that kind of thing to happen there. Obviously there is much more money avavilable in cricket, but I think it all comes down to thoughtfulness and communication. The official on that day appeared to have no capacity for thought at all. It was obscene.

Since the World Cup, and the marvellous job done by Phil Appleyard and his team, I have made a conscious effort to be constructive and helpful in whatever comments I have made. The interest in the game has continued to grow at a quite unprecedented rate with Los Angeles in 1984, the England silver medal in the World Cup, and now an Olympic gold – how many more opportunities does an association need to fully capitalise on its game?

The national club league, started in 1988, is a fantastic boost, but there are still only two clubs with their own artificial surfaces, Canterbury and Old Loughtonians. In Holland, however, every first- and second-division club had their own artificial pitch before 1984, as did teams in the German BundesLiga. Nowadays every Dutch first- and second-division club has *two* plastic pitches. That emphasises how far we have to go and how quickly we have to move. I think that we should be using a large portion of our sponsorship money to get people out into the streets to popularise the game. We should make sure that every child has the opportunity to get onto a pitch and try the game, and that there are no costs involved for him or her to do so.

I was invited to become a Minister's regional representative on the Sports Council in 1985, which made me consider that

81

some of the things that I was saying must have made some sense. Even though I have retired I will continue to study the development of the game and make constructive comments to improve it further.

The innovative national league has been received with much acclaim, but in a 'phone-in programme that I was involved in shortly after it started I got many callers asking where they could go to watch a game. I had to reply in general terms and advised them to 'phone local leisure centres, hockey players or even the Hockey Association, which wasn't terribly satisfactory. If you want to go and watch West Ham play or see Worcesterhire cricket at the county ground, there would be no such difficulty. The fixtures and venues are well publicised in advance and everyone knows when and where to go. I believe that our publicity must reach a wider audience and I'm sure that the recent appointment of Nick Irvine as Publicity and Marketing executive will help the situation enormously.

I often wonder what perception the ordinary man in the street and children have of the game, and I feel that this is another department which requires careful attention. How does the average club player feel? What is hockey's success doing for them? These are the people around whom the whole game is based. Every international has to build his career somewhere, and if we aren't looking after these grassroots players then the base on which our game is constructed will collapse. Despite all the lucrative sponsorship deals that are being signed how many children can go along to a centre and play a game? How many of the children who were bursting to play the game after we won the gold medal have been given the opportunity and encouraged to carry their ambitions further? What percentage have fallen away? Time is running out.

I suppose I'm critical because, although I've retired, hockey is inextricably a part of my life. I can't disassociate myself from the game that has been my love for so many years. There is nothing I would like more than to see Great Britain win the gold medal in Barcelona in 1992. But in addition I want the women to win the gold medal, and I'd like all of our teams to win the World Cups at senior and junior level and European Cups. I want success for us and I want to hear kids talking on high streets and in school playgrounds about the game. I want them to watch Sean Kerly play and be able to go out and emulate him. It's one of the few games in which boys and girls can relate to one another and play together without too many problems.

I've become a firm believer in the game and its positive effect on society. It is without doubt a clean family sport and there is no danger of hooliganism or other unpleasant spin-offs. The family participation, particularly on the continent, has shown me how enjoyable an occasion it can be. I've come full circle from playing as a carefree bachelor to seeing my sons imitating my medal-winning team-mates! We can enjoy the social involvements at the club as a family and that is what playing sport is all about. Sport should have a judicious mixture of fun, relaxation and competition, and I believe hockey provides exactly that.

However, as soon as we become complacent and accept that things are going well, then as far as I'm concerned that's a step backwards. I draw a parallel with my own game here – I've always said that I wanted every match to be better than the last one, and I believe that should also apply to the structure of hockey. I want more people enjoying the game, more playing it, more clubs, more families involved, more television coverage and more international tournaments at home! Even when I've faded out of the game I would love people coming into the game to derive as much enjoyment as I have without the unnecessary faults and hypocrisy that I've had to endure at times.

6
LOS ANGELES: BIRTH OF A REVOLUTION

For many people, Los Angeles was the start of our success. However, England and Great Britain teams had really been far more successful over the years than they had been given credit for. They had had a steady record of medal triumphs in major tournaments. I admit that there had ben a slight lull during the period when everyone was getting used to artificial surfaces, and both clubs and national players had to catch up as quickly as they could.

I believe that with this background in mind, that the achievements in 1984 were perhaps taken out of perspective. The media had never really followed hockey prior to this and when we were invited at the last minute it was a story that they eagerly grasped. Our non-qualification for the Games is a matter I have always felt strongly about, because it was decided purely on political grounds by the FIH who felt justified in inviting Malaysia for 'zonal or geographical' reasons. Our exclusion certainly didn't mean that we weren't good enough to be there in the first place, which is how the press portrayed it.

We were all confident in our inability when we set off, but the average man in the street was quite unaware of the background to it. There is no doubt that we were potential medal winners. Once we were there we began to play rather well, and it wasn't long before we had achieved a few victories. I think what appealed to the sporting media was that up until Los Angeles English teams had met with little success that year – the cricketers, rugby players and the like had not had good seasons. So when we started to win everyone sat up and began to take notice.

Sean Kerly and myself tended to be at the centre of the attention, which was a little unfair but inevitable because what happens in front of goal, be it the striker or the goalkeeper in action, tends to capture people's imagination. Sean had been converted from an inside-forward to a centre-forward at the tournament, and his incredible goal-scoring feats quickly catapulted him into the spotlight. As the Games progressed we carried on as we would in most competitions, quietly confident that we were still in with the chance of a medal.

Roger Self, our manager, found it difficult to cope with the sudden increase in media attention and tried to shield us from it altogether. That was probably quite a sensible move at the time because we were all very naive and could have been badly distracted by it. However, I still don't really believe he had the right to make that kind of unilateral decision, because we never actually realised how much attention was being paid to us. I know that when we arrived back after winning the bronze medal we were inundated with various requests but because of our inexperience it wasn't always easy to handle.

The focus of attention on us increased in Los Angeles when Princess Anne came to watch us, and we drew for the first time ever with Pakistan and finished top in our pool. We have always thought that the Princess Royal is our lucky mascot because in both Los Angeles and Seoul we never lost a game that she came to watch! In the semi-final we had the 'easier' of the matches, against West Germany, but that was our undoing. We learnt the hard way – there is no such thing as an 'easy' semi-final and they beat us. We were then pitted against Australia in the play-off for the bronze medal.

I recall that we were incredibly determined before the match, and we certainly had no idea how keenly the general public back in Britain were following our progress. Although the media had caught on to our achievements, they were apparently somewhat sceptical about our chances of beating the pre-tournament favourites. Our victory over Australia to take the bronze medal was enough to kindle everyone's imagination, and the supposed 'no hopers' were proclaimed as heroes. It was definitely one of the hardest matches I'd ever played in, and I know that the rest of the team found it equally gruelling.

It was the start of something most of us never dreamt could have happened. We arrived home to a rousing welcome at Heathrow and quite unbelievable media attention. It was only when I read through the press cuttings that I realised the sort of effect that our triumph had caused. It generated immense general interest, and a game that had previously been thought to have been played by girls and had been shunned by television and the media was now a great talking point. Although thousands of men and women played the game up and down the country, there had always been a sad lack of sponsorship and hockey had always been seen as a minor sport. But the public had now realised that it was a fast and exciting game, worth watching on TV. Thousands sat up waiting to watch the hockey at all sorts of unsociable hours – not just the British team but all the great hockey nations in action. I think that one of the disappointments was when hockey was scheduled for specific hours and then not shown for one reason or another.

Things snowballed after the publicity surrounding Los Angeles. One of the most important areas of improvement has been that of club hockey. Previously, club members would spend every weekend scrambling around on muddy pitches, playing a game that was totally divorced from that which the British team was playing. But through the marvellous increase in exposure, players across the country could see the style we were trying to achieve, and the metamorphosis that the game was undergoing. The change in goalkeeping appearances and methods, the return of the Indian dribble, the technique of flicking over huge distances and the faster speed of play made it not only a completely different game but made it a lot more fun as well. It gave people an incentive to go out and try it for themselves, and inspired them with something to aim for no matter what level they had been playing at.

The national team was elevated to new heights, and put upon a stage which had huge appeal to youngsters. Kids could now emulate their heroes and the public could identify hockey players. It was perceived as a game for the strong, fit and athletic and there was certainly nothing sissy about it. I think that was definitely a major breakthrough as far as hockey was concerned.

There were numerous examples of the wonderful effect it had on people. I was particularly struck by how quickly people passed over the congratulations and got onto the subject of hockey and how they could find out more about it. My local postmaster never used to watch hockey and only started to follow it on TV because he knew me. He was totally addicted to it on my return, and never stopped enthusing about it and comparing it to the football he watched thirty years ago! What he appreciated was not only the excitement and speed of the game, but how supporters from opposing teams sat with each other and actually laughed together!

The real tough nuts at school who had always been afraid to pick up a hockey stick and had played either football or rugby, suddenly started coming to me and asking about hockey. One lad sneaked up to me surreptiously at lunchtime one day and asked to join in the next game and so the examples went on. I remember one of the mothers telling me that her husband had been an ardent rugby fan for years and wouldn't have dreamt of letting his son play hockey, until one day the lad informed him that he wasn't going to the rugby club on Saturday but was off to hockey coaching instead! But having seen the Olympics his father was quite happy to let him make that choice.

There was also the lovely granny who raved about the game to me. I was helping with a presentation and the little granny told me that she watched an enormous amount of television and that of all the sports she'd watched hockey was by far the best. But what made me laugh were her comments on the physical characteristics of the players – especially Steve Batchelor's thighs!

All the comments amounted to a real increase in people's awareness of hockey, and it was a genuine eye-opener for other sports. If I had gone in to a local rugby club prior to the Games I would have been looked down on as a 'hockey player', but the difference in attitude was staggering after the Olympics. One of my first official events was a charity football for Children in Need, where I was asked to play goalkeeper in a celebrity football team. I think that was indicative of the recognition that hockey players were beginning to receive. Likewise the so-called specialist football commentators like David Icke, who covered little else at that time, began to take a great interest in hockey. He was very willing to learn all he could and was really enthusiastic about what he had seen in Los Angeles.

As I've said before, Sean Kerly and I tended to get most of the publicity and I couldn't help feeling sorry for someone like Jon Potter who had become the youngest British player ever to play in the Olympics and yet, despite that achievement and his splendid play, was almost completely overlooked on our return. All the midfield players who really set up most of the victories for the team were similarly ignored. It was the 'glory' positions of centre-forward and goalkeeper that attracted media attention. When events were organised we seemed to get the majority of the invitations, and of course that has a knock-on effect, and people became more and more inclined to continue inviting us.

We did the rounds of all the usual television programmes and appeared on several children's items as well. I enjoyed the charity side of it all, and we appeared on a very successful Children in Need fund raising day. Sean was sponsored for every goal he shot past me and I was sponsored for all those I saved. We were involved for quite a long period and we were both pretty tired by the end but it was certainly very worthwhile. When we had finished, I pulled off my sweat-soaked shirt and offered it for sale and got for £70 for it straightaway. I felt I couldn't have given my Olympic shirt away to a better cause.

Slowly Sean and I were both becoming personalities rather than interviewees and I think it's fair to say that we both enjoyed it. The revolution in LA had finally opened up the doors for hockey personalities to emerge, and I hope that continues for a long, long time to come. We still have to remind the general public about our sport and I think that this an important method of doing so.

What did seem to attract a lot of people was the Cinderella image of the game and the good clean family picture it presented. The players were model sportsman and although they were tough, fit and got stuck in, words like 'sorry', 'thank you' and 'excuse me' were still audible on the pitch. Despite the competitiveness there was no arguing with the umpires and the ball wasn't knocked 50 yards away at a free hit. It was something the public had tired of in football, and hockey provided a refreshing change. In contrast to football, hockey had an almost a fairy tale image and the top players weren't caught out up to no good in night clubs or mixed up in drug circles. In the true amateur spirit the players disregarded the sordid haggling over money and appearance fees and unselfishly promoted the game of hockey. Unfortunately because this attitude existed I believe that several interested sponsors ended up being turned away because of the incompetence of the HA.

The management style of the team went through a minor revolution and Roger Self was forced to give up several responsibilities, including coaching and selection, that he had previously been heavily involved in. The continual processes in the team's development meant that an effective and democratic system had to evolve. Senior players began to become much more involved, and the balance of power between the players, manager and coach resulted in the unqualified success in Seoul.

A lot of the ideas that helped to make the World Cup in London and Seoul so successful were actually formulated and implemented after the 1984 Olympics. I'm sure that the current HA President, Phil Appleyard, would have move things into action a lot sooner but his first responsibility was the World Cup and he was only elected to the HA in 1985. Packed stands, friendly scenes, great competition, excitement and national pride during the World Cup spurred on renewed media coverage and again the tabloids turned out in force. There were even ticket touts, and seats for the final and semi-finals were being exchanged for outrageous sums of money. That raised the big question – could we get a bigger stadium for the next time and the time after that? It was without doubt one of the best-run hockey tournaments I've ever played in, and we all have a lot to thank Phil and his team for.

Outstanding individual performances by certain players during the World Cup helped to shift the focus of attention from Sean and myself to people like Imran Sherwani, Norman Hughes, Steve Batchelor and Paul Barber. However the media still appeared to target Sean and me, and there was a certain amount of resentment amongst the other players. A decision was then made that whenever possible other players would be used at press conferences, so that they became used to being spokesmen for the team and projecting their own personalities.

I've enjoyed enormously all the opportunities that have opened up for me since I won the gold medal. By that I don't just mean from a sports angle, but all sorts of things that are nothing to do with hockey. Simple things like launching the local poppy appeal or lighting a bonfire to help raise £700 for the local hospice, have meant a great deal to me. People do need publicity for good causes, and I've loved being able to help.

What we have to consider seriously is how best to keep the press involved and ensure that the media maintain their enthusiasm for the game. There is no violence, booing or shouting in the stands and few controversial incidents on the pitch. I think the worst thing that happened in the World Cup was an argument in the one of the bars in a marquee. Apparently it was between two chaps, about who was buying the next round, and set up for the benefit of the press who duly raced over to report the supposed 'brawl!'

Because of the parlous state of English sport at the moment, I believe that the hockey administrators should be well prepared for any ugly incidents. I don't think they should wait for the problems to arise, but should be ready and able to deal with bad or violent behaviour on the spot. People should be made well aware that hockey is not prepared to accept the abominable behaviour that has crept into other games.

There are now many areas where the game has developed and will continue to develop. We've broken away from the tradition stronghold of local and centralised leagues and are in the midst of a highly successful national league structure. In the long run that is fantastic for the game because the top players now face each other on a a regular basis on artificial pitches every week throughout the country. A negative aspect is that points won or lost in each encounter are crucial, and will become increasingly so, leading to hotly contested matches and cut-throat competitiveness.

One issue I feel very strongly about is that hockey is first and foremost a family game, and that the club game should produce a family environment. Yet so many of the national league club sides rarely get the opportunity to experience this side of the game, because not only do their teams not have the facilities, but they spend most of their weekends travelling up and down motorways with few occasions to stay behind in a clubhouse. Consequently the first eleven members seldom socialise with or get to know the other players in either their clubs or those of the opposition. I know of teams that have never been to their opponent's clubhouse simply because it may be twenty minutes down the road in the wrong direction and so they prefer to set off immediately to the next venue. If they do get back to their own clubhouse it's late at night and most of the regular members have long since left.

I hope that club loyalty doesn't fade and that we avoid the 'what club are you playing for this season?' situation. There is one chap I know of who is at his fifth club in five seasons and

I think that sort of development is bad for the game. Good as the national league is, the club system has always been founded on loyalty, friendship and close links between players of all abilities. The 'superstars' should never be isolated from the grassroots supporters.

The unpleasant side to a competitive league, like players being sent off and warned, is already beginning. You get that sort of thing when the game is isolated into one performance rather than a continuing representation. If you're representing your club or country there is a certain pride associated with it, but if you are merely going through the motions and only thinking of winning you tend to forget the pride aspect. Of course there are other by-products of this kind of exposure, like one's past performances and personal life being scrutinised by the media. I think it's an area in which players have to be extremely circumspect.

The developments over the last decade have been quite fascinating and in many ways I can see a reflection of the men's game in women's hockey. Much of what we did several years ago is now being done in the women's game, and they seem to have undergone a similar period of development in both playing styles and administration. It's interesting how my view of women's hockey has changed, from the traditional picture of overweight women trundling around a muddy pitch, to the impressive sight of the Dutch ladies in action, which I saw at one of my first international tournaments in Holland.

At the time I pondered how far apart the women's games in Holland and Great Britain were. But as I thought about it I wondered whether the British women's team were trying to emulate the men in the same way that other men's nations were looking to us. Maybe one day they will also be world beaters. I've always looked at hockey as one game, and believe that whatever the men do reflects on the women and vice versa. I can remember the days when hockey received hardly any publicity but the names of Rachael Heyhoe Flint and Val Robinson and their hockey achievements were bandied about more than any hockey players – men or women.

I think it's a great shame that the two governing bodies continue to operate separately. I'm ignorant of the politics involved but the strength in numbers could, I'm sure, carry hockey to much greater heights. I also believe that the ladies' approaches for financial help would be much more successful if they were able to present their case from a position of strength in numbers. In all honesty when I see the women and the men play at the top levels there is no difference, the only discrepancy is in the coaching methods and the mental attitude. Just as the British men's team developed a successful style of play in the years preceding Seoul, I see no reason why women's teams can't do the same. The key issue is using the depth of experience available effectively rather than arguing and playing political games.

I think that the men's bronze medal in 1984 was regarded somewhat jealously by some of the ladies and particularly by the administration. They saw a lot of finance suddenly being channelled into the men's game, and although they still had enormously popular events like the Wembley internationals I think some of them resented it. Some of the promising young players and coaches have been lost because of the attitude of some of the administrators, and selectors who haven't kept in touch with the game's developments. If they really want to capitalise on the success of the men's game, then I believe the women's administration should undergo radical improvements.

The women have the potential to produce superb teams and follow in the men's steps, but the difference between winning a medal and not is vast. Everyone will remember where the men ended up in Seoul, but it's doubtful that many will recall the women's final position in two or three years' time. Although they performed as best they could, they didn't quite make it when it counted and that is what they will have to work on. I feel that the women should liaise closely with the men to establish their common objectives and move forward together. An ideal way for the two associations to work more closely would be to stage international fixtures at the same venue whenever possible. For example, the match between the Great Britain men's side and the rest of Europe at Luton to celebrate the gold medal could very easily have included a women's match which could drawn a much larger audience. But it wasn't done. Why? Why are details of new coaching schemes only circulated to the men's clubs? Obviously it's because they aren't affiliated and why should they all affiliate to two associations? But that is where the communication breaks down.

We seem to be duplicating resources when we should all have the same objectives. If you look at the highly successful Dutch system, men and women come under the same umbrella. The duplication of resources is one of the absurd problems that could be overcome. Instead of sending out two sets of details concerning coaching or umpiring schemes as happens now, there need only be one mailing list co-ordinated from one central office. Instead of applications for financial help to lay artificial surfaces being sent in by both associations, and almost in competition with one another, a merged body would almost certainly have greater success. Obviously there would have to be extensive negotiations and co-operation to iron out the intricate details but I can't help believing that if hockey is to continue to progress then this is the best way forward.

If the game isn't bigger than the arguments between men and women, and controversy amongst clubs administrators and players, then ultimately hockey will be the loser. This conflict permeates up to the national levels where we have a Welsh, Scottish and Irish hockey associations plus a Great Britain men's and a Great Britain women's board. If that confuses the hockey world in Britain, it's not surprising that the international organisers are never quite sure who they are dealing with or sending invitations to. Do they invite Britain or England, men and women, is it Scotland or should Wales be included? It's ridiculous.

Obviously such a system instils national pride in players and exposes far more players to the game, but in fact one association would give that opportunity to everyone anyway. It could all be run through one administration working effectively and efficiently. Although the home countries could keep their separate identities, one association could ensure that, for example, England's outdoor success could help Scotland's indoor. Unfortunately there are too many people concerned with their own power struggles to concede, and therefore we will never have a united front.

One of the developments associated with the game and the subsequent establishment of the national league is the emergence of the transfer fee. I often wonder how long this will take and I am taking a keen interest in what has been happening. We've certainly seen it in other sports but of course those are professional games. I don't think that hockey could ever be supported as a professional game in Britain, and I am strongly opposed to the concept. The principle of why people play the game would be overthrown, the game would end up moving further and further away from the very things that made it popular in the first place. Besides the inevitable outrageous demands made by players over money, it could lead to all the professional fouls and abuse of referees that have given football such an appalling image. The tactical game would be much more in evidence, and the reasons of playing for pure enjoyment and relaxation would become a sad memorial of the past.

The success of the Great Britain men's team in Seoul would never have received the acclaim it did if we have achieved it through poor, professional and ill-tempered tactics. An example of that was in the football World Cup when Maradona cheated against England. His team may have won but it certainly left everyone with a very bad taste in their mouths. It's imperative that administrators make absolutely clear what direction they want the game to take and the type of behaviour that will or will not be be tolerated. It's inevitable that at some stage someone will be offered money to change clubs or will receive some kind of financial reward for scoring goals, and I feel that hockey administrators should be well prepared to handle the situation when it arises.

I know from personal experience that after I had announced my retirement I had several offers to go and play for various clubs. I'm not prepared to name them but in a couple of the offers I was given assurances of substantial financial rewards. That would have been unthinkable a few years ago, but the increased sponsorship at a local level has made it possible. Undoubtedly that will be prevalent throughout the country but a strong and effective system implemented by the HA should discourage it. One way would be to ban players from playing for two national league clubs within two years of each other. I know there would be cases where someone might have genuine reasons for moving from one part of the country to another, but my personal opinion is that he should then be forced to play for the second team.

Another notable development that has resulted from the revolution in hockey is the coaching of children. Local club coaches and regional coaches have made enormous strides in spreading the gospel to youngsters throughout the country, and the improvements have been dramatic. When I think back to how raw the Batchelors and Kerlys were when they first came through the system, the difference now is incredible. They had undeniable talent but nowhere near the skill that so many players possess today. I'm sure that without the success of the national team all those working at the lower coaching levels would never have had the enthusiasm or directive to produce what they have. Russell Garcia, the 18-year-old who won a gold medal in Seoul, is a shining example of how quick progress has been.

Watching a schoolboy match these days is a revelation, and I think that applies equally to schoolgirl hockey. I umpired a county girls' match when I returned from Seoul and the standard was astounding. It can only have been the success of the respective national sides that has encouraged them to achieve those standards so early on in their development. One of the greatest things is that children have now been given the opportunity, through all the publicity, to go and imitate their heroes. I noticed that the girls I was umpiring did just that, and when one of them scored they all ran back to the middle saying 'Annette Sixsmith has scored – she's our answer to Sean Kerly!'

I sometimes wonder, though, whether all the available talent has been utilised. Of course my ideal would be for all of England's teams, men and women, across all the age groups, to win every tournament possible, and then for the British sides to win the gold medal in Barcelona, and in 1996, and so on. However I do believe it will be difficult for the national senior team to follow the Seoul success, because that was achieved through years of experience. I doubt whether there will be enough occasions for teams to gather the colossal amount of experience and implement it successfully.

The squad that started the ball of fortune rolling in 1984 was a unique blend of players. They formulated their own team character and worked tirelessly towards a common objective for nearly eight years. I think the pressure is on all international teams now to do the same, and the only way that they can possibly succeed is to adopt a novel and distinctive approach. The younger players coming into the senior ranks have immense talent and vision but they haven't yet developed the burning ambition that is required at top level – something all of the 1988 squad possessed in excessive quantities.

It's essential to look forward to the World Cup and Barcelona. Hopefully there will be several of the Seoul team members in those squads to help guide the less experienced lads, but I am concerned about the lack of time there is left to prepare them for these daunting tasks. There are bound to be comparisons with the well-known players who have since retired, and it's important that the new players don't pay too much attention to their critics and get on with the job as best they can. I'm glad that there were no such pressures in my early days, and because I was never in the public eye I had the chances to experiment, adapt, improve my techniques and gain experience.

I believe that it is absolutely imperative that a national team coach is appointed who is independent of any other activities. The game can't afford to have somebody trying to do two jobs like David Whitaker did – who was national director of coaching and national coach. One of the major reasons he was successful was the mixture of players he had at the time, namely English internationals. We need a cold, calculating opinion expressed by an individual who is totally independent. A national director of coaching must be concerned primarily with bringing through the next generation of coaches. The problem, of course, will be whether the administration deem it viable to spend money on giving young coaches every available opportunity to prepare for the future.

It's the old point of speculating before accumulating and if we want to prosper in the future there has to be investment now. One of the great bones of contention will be umpires, and I think they are in an unenviable situation. They often have to put up with abuse and are seldom appreciated, but the game can't survive without them. Umpires should be encouraged much more and I would love to see young people taking it up rather than players who have retired picking up whistles. Let's have 20-year-olds and under-16s becoming interested. I can recall an 18-year-old Dutch umpire at a tournament once and that's just the sort of enterprise that we should be showing. Unfortunately the system sticks with a few umpires for year after year, and only when they depart from the scene do the next generation come through. There should be an innovative scheme for continuity. If players are expected to perform well at all levels from national league to international then they must have umpires of a particular standard whom they respect. It's when certain umpires are regarded as 'jokes' that standards start to deteriorate.

At the moment I think the rules of the game are well thought out and in the interest of hockey. The individuality of the penalty corner makes it stand out from other games and the penalty stroke also carries a lot of curiosity. Perhaps there could be slight adaptations in the rules for mini-hockey which would help children derive a great deal more from their introduction to the game. It's possible that goalkeeping styles will alter between now and the next Olympics because of a rule change and I think that many more 'keepers will revert to a more upright stance in the next major tournament. By constantly reviewing the rules I think that we can keep in touch with the development of the game. But obviously it mustn't be change for the sake of it.

Since Los Angeles an enormous amount of lessons have been learnt and a great deal of positive changes and advances have been made. All that has meant that there is a vast pool of experience now available amongst players, coaches, umpires and management and I think it's essential that it isn't all lost. The best possible use should be made of all the experience, and people like Richard Dodds who has been a World Cup, Great Britain and Olympic captain have immense amounts of knowledge to pass on. He is one of the finest representatives of the game that we have ever had. I do tend to think that we don't make enough use of such valuable resources which are vital in any success. I can remember early on in my career feeling very disassociated from the national team and I wouldn't like to see that happening again. A feeling of belonging is one of the most important aspects of success. I saw arrogant athletes at the Olympics who wouldn't even sign autographs, and some self-styled heroes in England tell you to talk to their manager at the slightest request – I hope that never happens in hockey.

The game must continue to go forward. I would like to see the teams carrying on successfully and I would love to see a system of club hockey similar to that on the continent. Families and children should be the focal point in the club, and married women should be able to play sport in a friendly atmosphere and where there is no bias against children, boys, girls or whatever. I think that there should be one board completely in control of British hockey but most of all I would like to see the traditional amateur principles of the game preserved.

7
AROUND THE
WORLD IN 12 YEARS

In the twelve years that I was lucky enough to play international hockey I travelled to many countries all around the world, and have a vivid recollection of many aspects of life in them. Some of the countries have been, and still are, major forces in the hockey world, but others have been attractive to me for a variety of reasons.

AUSTRALIA

I suppose I should start with Australia who have been ranked number one in several Olympics, but who have have always faltered and have yet to better their silver medal in the 1976 Montreal Games when they were beaten by New Zealand. I do believe that the competition is so strong nowadays that being ranked number one can sometimes be misleading. Quite often any one of a number of teams is capable of winning the tournaments. Australia are an enigma to themselves because they have never achieved what everyone expects them to. Despite their disappointing Olympic record, the Australians have an impressive record of achievements and, along with West Germany, are the only team to have won the prestigious Champions Trophy four successive times. They are also the current World Champions.

I think one of the reasons for their success is that they play a very fast, direct game which is effective because all of their players are natural athletes and because they are very familiar with one another's play. Almost every move is pre-determined. This clinical pattern, however, is probably also their stumbling-block. Whilst they have exciting forwards, they don't actually possess flair, and I know that whenever one of them comes into the circle he has practised the move hundreds of times in training. He will do exactly the same thing every time, and won't try anything innovative. Teams who beat them have worked out a formula that can cope with this stereotyped play and are prepared to be adventurous in an attempt to break up their pattern.

Their basic philosophy is to get the ball from the defence to the forwards as quickly as possible, with the rest of the team moving up in support. But this leaves enormous gaps at the back, and skilful forwards can always work their way through which is just what Sean Kerly, Steve Batchelor and Imran Sherwani did in the semi-final in Seoul with huge success. Their right-half had been so used to following up close behind his front runners that when our strikers exploited the offside rule and positioned themselves right up on the 25-yard line, he was nowhere in sight. The result was that the full backs were forced to come across in cover, opening up even more gaps for us!

The unorthodox will always unsettle them and at the crucial moments they don't have the flair and imagination to overcome unfamiliar tactics by opponents.

The hockey set-up in Australia is very different to the British system. For a start, it is a huge country and there is a four hour time difference between east and west coasts. It's a two day coach ride from north to south and obviously such massive mileages make inter-state games infrequent and difficult to stage. Therefore, hockey is concentrated very much within the states with club sides playing one another two or three times in a season. The government has realised the political value of sporting success and have ploughed vast sums in to the game. The Australian Institute of Sport is a university-type organisation where promising young hockey players are given the opportunity to improve their game but can also work at the same time. There are two institutes, one in Perth – the major one for hockey – and one in Canberra. Facilities are fantastic and it means the national coaches can get hold of players coming through very early on and achieve a degree of continuity throughout the system.

It's also interesting how closely together the men and women work and both teams have an almost identical style of play. Richard Aggiss, the amiable men's national coach for many years, must take a lot of the credit for Australia's success over the last decade. He has ensured continuity by appointing past international players such as Terry Walsh to coach at the National Institute of Sport. Players are often selected for the institute after they are 'spotted' at the inter-state tournament which is certainly the most important in their calendar and one where the national hopefuls are picked out.

I have always thought the Australian administration not only very efficient and professionally run but relaxed as well. The professional trappings are also very much in evidence and as far back as 1979 the Australian players were being given as much as A$40 a day in expenses at tournaments. I remember when we toured Australia once we played a test in Sydney and a week later were due to play another test in Melbourne. Peter Haselhurst, one of their players, should have flown back to Perth and then returned the following week. But the Australian Association decided that it would probably work out cheaper and be better for him if he was sent on a skiing holiday in the mountains instead. Most of us in the England team couldn't believe it – his holiday was actually paid for! But of course it was an extremely sensible idea and naturally it helped him to perform better.

I know that all their international players are well looked after and in the early days before Richard Charlesworth became a Federal MP and was a doctor in a hospital, he was rarely seen in the wards! For certain people in this country that would cause a few raised eyebrows but I think when the sport is an amateur one, everyone needs to have the backing and understanding of authorities and it will never get anywhere unless this is the case. It wasn't long before several British players were attracted by the lifestyle and commitment to the game in Australia and emigrated. Flights were paid for, jobs were found, cars were supplied and although a lot of people found it distasteful it was all in the interests of promoting the game.

I've been to Australia at least eight times and I think it's an absolutely beautiful country. It's hard to envisage what a huge and diverse country it is. On one of my earlier tours to Australia, and the first time I went to Darwin, I went to try and overcome jet lag and get in some practice on a dusty and deserted field. One of the other players came to shoot at me and I dived and threw myself all over the place until I was quite exhausted. I went off to go and collect the balls which had gone into a marshy sort of woodland and hoped it would give me some breathing space. It was then that I noticed an Australian sitting with his feet up in the back of his jeep, drinking a can of lager, with corks in his hat and all! He shouted out nonchalantly to me: 'Don't go in there 'keeper – there's crocodiles mate!'

It's a lovely story – I never did wait to find out if he was telling the truth or not!

It would be unfair to say that I've seen much of Australia because as I've said earlier, what I'm most familiar with are the airports, hockey pitches and hotels. But in the times I have managed to get out and see the sights I've been most impressed. Sydney is very cosmopolitan but Canberra has very little atmosphere. Melbourne is similar to old England and I think all the crazy fruitcakes in Australia have emigrated to Tasmania! They're lovely fun loving people but a completely different brand to Australians. South Australians appear much more sombre and serious, but I think that once you get to know them they are probably a lot more sincere than the Western Australians who, being a more transient population, tend to be rather more shallow.

The outstanding characteristics of Australians are their love of beer and their preoccupation with 'Pommie bashing'! Australians are more nationalistic than any other folk I have ever played against. If the Poms are playing then they will pull out all the stops to beat us – especially in Australia. All the rugby, cricket and hockey contests are close but despite all the joking and ribbing beforehand, the Australians are the first to have a drink with you afterwards and are great company.

I used to eat lobster in any shape or form on tours. So much so that the team used to ask me if I was having it for breakfast! But I've also tried the other seafood delicacies and of course have had the usual thick steaks and all that goes with a typically huge Aussie breakfast! I'm sure that eating so much meat has something to do with the robust and brawny build of most Australians. The barbecues are another aspect of their lifestyle that I thoroughly enjoy, and I always found their informal nature terribly conducive to socialising and getting to know people. In many ways I envy the relaxed way of life the Australians lead, but it's really only made possible by the marvellous climate they have.

HOLLAND

I suspect that anyone who plays top-class hockey or is connected with the game would have visited Holland more than any other country. The reason is that they are extremely organised and successful and put on more tournaments than any other nation. Although football is their major sport, hockey is very definitely one of their national games and has a tremendous following. Because of its high profile, you can always bet quite safely that if Holland are playing an important international then it will be sell-out.

Their astonishing club system has ensured that there is huge participation at all levels in the game. Entire families belong to clubs and playing hockey is an enjoyable and accepted way of life. The social environment of the clubs means that other sports may be played, but they attract people with good restaurants, bars and a healthy image. Such a system provides enormous depth and there is a continuous striving for success. Youngsters are coached by excellent coaches and all aspects of the game are well looked after. Again, several British players have gone to Holland and are making a living from hockey.

There have been rumblings on the circuit about Dutch players benefiting financially from the sport and there was one occasion when the entire national team turned out in different shoes for a game because they all had varying sponsors! The Association took a strong line and instructed all the players that one of the terms of selection was that they accepted whatever kit had been agreed on and that such behaviour would not be tolerated in future. There has been so such incident since!

The Dutch have been able, with the interest and financial support, to set up a very successful system. Because it isn't a huge country it is far easier for the Dutch players to meet each other on frequent occasions. For a player based in Amsterdam, for instance, it would be possible to play any other side in the country within approximately an hour and a half. And that sort of convenience has meant the growth of the powerful Dutch club system. It has also assisted the coaching programme, and naturally it has been relatively simple to co-ordinate and implement national coaching schemes.

Holland's success has been based on whatever was most efficient at the time in the game. For a long time it was the penalty corner with the men, and of course still is with the women. Individuals like Paul Litjens and Ties Kruize, and to a lesser extent Jan Floris Bovelander, have dominated this particular aspect of the game for years. They don't play the free running game like the Australians, but a far more disciplined one with a couple of forwards running free up front. I was always wary of Dutch forwards because they had this uncanny knack of putting the ball in the back of the net from the most obscure places and from the acutest of angles. They were usually fast, skilful and possessed plenty of flair.

I often wondered why they were such superb finishers and it was when I played in one tournament that the answer became apparent. During the half-time break hundreds of young children would rush out onto the pitch and practise an amazing array of shots in the goalmouths. There wasn't a reverse flick scoop, push, chip or shot they couldn't do and their enthusiasm was infectious. I'm sure they were imitating their heroes and it was quite plain that there is nothing that Dutch children like more than scoring goals. That sort of practice is so important for building up the familiarity with the hockey stick and how it can be used. English children do the same with a football, kicking it around for hours on end and performing all the tricks they can with it. Hockey is fun and I firmly believe that all practices should incorporate these tricks and odd diversions. That's why Dutch children are so good at hockey and at the end of the day after school, they go off to a club. It's something that every British teacher should think about.

Holland is a delight to travel to not only because of the Dutch players' and officials' attitude to hockey but also because of the public's enthusiastic response to it. The players in the 1988 Olympic squad were given every Tuesday, Wednesday and Thursday afternoon off by their employers to train in Amsterdam for nearly a year preceding the 1988 Olympics. In addition to this they were given every Monday off as a rest day because obviously they had been playing in strenuous matches over the weekend! I think that this paid dividends and from being ranked well below their normal expectations, they won the bronze medal. I think that sort of approach is the only way to succeed.

Holland is one country I would be very happy to visit time and time again. They love to eat good restaurant food and I thoroughly enjoy the atmosphere in the bars where everyone is friendly and relaxed. Of course I love Dutch beers – although we were never allowed to over-indulge in recent years! But I do remember in years gone by, when we had a much weaker side, that the highlight of the tour would be evenings in the bar after matches! Another little indulgence of mine is chips dipped into hot peanut butter sauce, which they serve in cafés over there. The first time I discovered this I think I put on about two pounds in as many days!

The atmosphere in the Wagener Stadium in Amstelveen near Amsterdam must be one of the best in the world. The Dutch are fiercely patriotic and, with the stands filled to capacity, they set up the familiar chant: 'Holland, Holland!' At half time there is a flurry of activity on to the pitch with every child who has brought a stick with him or her charging out to practise. I wish more British kids did that. The other remarkable thing about Amstelveen is that you see whole families sitting together in the stands – from granny and grandpa right down to babies in arms. It doesn't mean that any of their family are playing, they just go for a pleasurable outing.

PAKISTAN

After Holland, I think my most visited country is Pakistan where apart from playing in numerous testimonial and exhibition matches I have competed in several Champions' Trophies. Although I say Pakistan it's been mainly the cities of Karachi, Islamabad and Lahore with the odd fleeting visit to other areas. When you consider that Pakistan is a relatively new country it has made very quick progress in quite a short period after the British introduced hockey on the sub-continent.

I think that it caught on so quickly because apart from the similarities with cricket – that is hitting a round object with an implement – the Asian physique is ideally suited to the skills required in hockey. With their lithe, athletic build they had little difficulty responding to the lightning movements and wrist mobility in hockey. They took to hockey naturally and it's not unusual to see children playing hockey in the streets all over the country. The rather poor pitches they had to play on actually helped them develop their skills to a high degree, and when it came to playing on good, true surfaces their formidable repertoire came to the fore.

It wasn't really any wonder that India and Pakistan dominated world hockey for such a long time. Hockey players are given the same sort of royal treatment that is reserved for people like Imran Khan in the cricket arena these days, and the rewards offered to hockey players ensured a steady stream of players into the game. Major companies support the sport with enormous sums of money and national training centres are organised for players to attend. These centres can run for eight or nine months of the year and any player attending would be excused from working but would receive full pay. I know of one forward at the Seoul Olympics who had received three promotions in the last three years but had never been into the office! The reason for this advancement was that his team had won three tournaments!

Everyone knows that this sort of thing goes on and it is accepted that, like cricketers, national hockey players are national heroes. The financial resources have meant that massive stadiums have been built and artificial surfaces have been put down. The one in Karachi is magnificent and must seat about 75,000 people. It's the Wembley of hockey, with every conceivable facility. With such favourable circumstances it's not difficult to see why Pakistan and India reigned supreme for so long in the world of hockey. But it couldn't last.

Pakistan are hardly down and out of world hockey but they have had a variety of results in recent years ranging from first to last in tournaments. The reason, I believe, is that the turnover of players has been too quick and that they have failed to maintain a balance between experience and youth. Too many of their best players have left the game very early in their careers, or they've become greedy and others haven't trained hard enough to keep up with the tough physical demands of today's game. Pakistan seem to appear with a new team every couple of years, and although they are skilful and capable they are certainly not tournament-hardened. And

I think that has a lot to do with their disappointing form in the World Cup of 1986 and the the 1988 Olympics. In a one-off game situation, however, there is no doubt that Pakistan could beat any side in the world today.

Karachi is a frenetic, cosmopolitan city where everything seems to go by a whir! One of the former World Cup and Olympic captains, Islah-Uddin, had a benefit game to mark his retirement and Pakistan International Airways flew me out. When I arrived I was looked after extremely well and given the best possible treatment. There were 76,000 people in the stands, live television coverage, and we were fêted whenever we went. I think the match ended in an honourable draw and after the reception we went up to Islah's house. It was in a fashionable area of Karachi and I remember that the living room had five enormous windows in the shape of the Olympic rings! The residence was a present on his retirement and apparently he also received a substantial sum of money from all the fund-raising events. Rumour has it that President Zia made a personal donation and there were others from ministers in the government. It was considered quite normal that a national hero should be afforded such comforts on his retirement and that he fully deserved to be comfortable for the rest of his life. He is still very active in the affairs of Pakistani hockey either as a reporter or as part of the team management. That sort of money would be unheard of in England unless it was in football or cricket and I think it shows the difference between the sport in the two countries.

It's a bold thing to say and rather general, but I think that the Asian attitude to sport has led them to become very critical of themselves and perhaps expect too much. It could be that they are aware of the rewards and are trying to achieve success in order to reap the rich financial security at the end of it all. I've been involved in matches where we've beaten Pakistan and the immediate response of the crowd has been to hurl the closest missiles to hand at the Pakistan team. The fact that they had lost honourably never came into it, it was that the national pride had been severely wounded and their superiority had been challenged. On the other hand, I remember travelling back with the Pakistan team after they had won the World Cup in Bombay because I had been invited to play in another benefit match for one of their players. They were driven back from the airport in an open-top bus, and the route into Karachi – about ten miles – was lined with thousands upon thousands of cheering fans. The day was declared a national holiday and money was thrown into containers like dustbins hanging on the side of the bus. On arriving in the city centre they were given a heroes' welcome and lauded all day long. To think it was a hockey team – it was quite amazing to me! I received some spin-off from all the euphoria and was put up in the best hotel and was given every possible luxury.

The players duly received ample financial rewards and pieces of land. I know that several of them would never have to work again because they were so well looked after – which is what benefits are supposed to ensure. I consider a lot of them very good friends of mine, and I believe that Pakistan has made a major contribution to world hockey and will continue to do so.

WEST GERMANY

There is absolutely no doubt in my mind that the West Germans have been the most consistent hockey team in my playing career. They are one of the best tournament teams that I've ever played against, and although their results have varied, they have rarely finished out of the top four. Germany have a thoroughly professional approach and have always made the most of their resources. I think that one of the reasons for their success is their long-serving coach, Klaus Kleiter, whom I hold in great esteem. Kleiter has done both German and world hockey a huge service and there can't be many coaches who haven't learnt from him. His enterprise and foresight in bringing through young players is widely acknowledged and he is an expert in 'blooding' them and preparing them for their senior international careers. Good examples are Thomas Reck and Andreas Keller who are two current German internationals, but both in their early 20s with at least 100 caps each. Their potential was quickly identified by Kleiter who gave them ten or fifteen minutes on the pitch at a time, put no pressure on them and now they are well established regulars in the side.

Apart from bringing through the youngsters and forming a good solid base for German hockey, he also utilises every bit of relevant information he can in preparing his team. Whether it's to do with diet, training, coaching methods or psychological approaches, the chances are that Klaus will be aware of it. In addition to all that he is always very much in control of the tactical side of the game, and the German efficiency and ruthlessness enables his masterplans to be carried out. I know that the players have the highest regard and respect for him.

I love the challenge of facing West Germany and have had many exciting and memorable matches against them. The irony is that Germany is the only team ever to have beaten us in an Olympic Games that I've played in – once in Los Angeles and once in Seoul. But it is that twist of fate that makes me smile when I think back to our victory over them in the 1988 Olympic final.

Like the Dutch, the Germans have a very strong club system but I don't think it's quite as family-orientated. Of course they do have much greater distances to travel for their matches and it's normal for three clubs to meet at a venue over one weekend and play two games. I think this stands them in good stead for typical tournament play and their players must find it easy to adapt to playing two or three successive games rather than the one-off situation. The harsh winters force the Germans indoors for four months and as I understand it they now break their hockey season in two parts, playing from August to the end of October and from April to June.

It would be fair to say that the popularity of the game in Germany has had its ups and downs and generally, there seems to be more public support for the indoor game. A lot of sponsorship appears to come from their national indoor league and there is no doubt that they have dominated the indoor game, both men and women, for a long time. The German women seem to have deteriorated a bit in recent years. I have always considered them to be the only force likely to challenge the Dutch but now it's the Australians and Koreans. Perhaps it's because the women have a much greater diversity of sports to choose from and they tend to play lots of other games at top level.

As I've said the Germans are incredibly professional – and that includes travelling with a huge stock of delicacies that they particularly enjoy! Whenever we went on tour I would scrounge meats and black bread from either Stefan Bloecher or Heiner Dopp, who always had well-stocked fridges in their rooms. Unfortunately though, I haven't really played many tournaments in Germany and when we have played the Germans it's tended to be a case of flying in, having a couple of matches and taking the next plane out again.

Generally, I've got a lot of time for the Germans – they're honest, frank, keep to their word and are warm and open-hearted. I've got more German friends from the international hockey circuit than any other country which shows my affection for them.

INDIA

A lot of what I've said about Pakistan probably applies to India but of course it is a much larger land mass and distances are immense. I think their resources are slightly more restricted although the backing from the top is still very strong. Their demise has been due almost entirely to a lack of artificial surfaces although I think they now have three or four. It makes it very difficult for players to get to so few but again, like Pakistan, once players are selected they go to a national training camp and are established on the pitches as an almost full-time job.

They have incredible skill but not the depth of fitness, and they also have a complicated political system to cope with.

These differences are reflected in the selection and playing procedures, and certain religions have been known to have been discriminated against in selection. This has caused a considerable amount of turmoil and changes at all levels are constantly being rung in order to overcome the complex internal bickering. If a lack of artificial pitches could be a factor in their downfall, then so could the way the buck is constantly being passed. Fingers were pointed in every conceivable direction after Seoul, and the whole system was all but destroyed.

But an Indian team will always thrill spectators with their stickwork, wizardry and their deft body swerves. The speed with which they convert from defence to attack is another attractive side to their game, and they also have a mischievous confidence in their own ability where they almost taunt the opposition to rob them of the ball!

One of the most memorable experiences of my life happened in India and by that I don't mean achieving a gold medal. In 1977 when we toured India I was quite young and impressionable and trying to establish myself on the international circuit. One day we had to catch the overnight first-class train from Bombay to our destination which was some considerable distance away. We took all our bags down to the station ready to load in to the respective compartments. I had a simply huge bag in those days and it had been nicknamed Bertha! It was about five foot long, just under three foot wide and about the same height. When full it was practically impossible to lift!

It carried all my equipment and all my personal belongings on the tour. We arrived at the platform and the bags were about to be loaded onto the train when we realised that we were on the wrong platform and would have to go over a bridge to get to our correct train. The Indians insisted that we couldn't carry our own bags and went off to fetch some porters for us. One delightful little chap, who looked about sixty, arrived to help and, with a neat swing and flick of his wrists hoisted my bag up on to his head! I was even more amazed when he took his hands away and the bag remained perfectly balanced! But what really astounded us was when he asked that John Hurst's bag (which was identical to mine) to be put on top of mine. Despite our protests he insisted, and when we relented this wizened little man walked along the platform, up the steps, over the bridge and deposited our things on the correct train! The tip I gave him was nothing by our standards, but he was quite overwhelmed, which really brought home the gulf between our different ways of life.

The train was far from luxurious and inside the compartment the beds were boards that folded down and were attached at one end by a chain. And as I unwound the bed roll, several little cockroaches jumped out and ran away. We all decided that the duty-free drinks we had bought would be consumed as quickly as possible in that first hour! The toilet was a hole in the floor and it didn't take long for all of us to realise that travelling in India was going to be an interesting experience!

When we arrived one of the Indians on the train came round and asked if any of us wanted tea. I said that I did and he took out what was obviously a cherished china tea pot and then walked up to the engine which was two carriages away, turned on a tap at the side of the steam engine, poured in the boiling water – and there was the tea! Another chap offered me boiled eggs which I thought would be a good idea and so off he went with his little pot to boil them in. Again from the engine! As I was eating the eggs it suddenly stuck me that at no stage had I come across a yolk and the whole egg was completely white. It was pointed out to me that this was not the case and it did in fact have one, but because the chicken had been so undernourished it was scarcely visible.

We played one game in a huge stadium with the pitch right in the middle and people sitting everywhere. Apparently there were around 100,000 spectators and they were perched in the most spectacular places in and around the stadium in an attempt to get a good view. The majority had travelled there by bicycle and when we tried to leave the stadium there was such chaos that the only way out was for all the England team to jump on a bike each and pedal furiously to the coach. As we leaped onto the coach, the driver set off like a maniac, thumb on the horn, foot hard down on the accelerator and we must have left a trail of ruined bicycles and spectators in our wake as we tore back to our hotel!

We visited magnificent sights like the Taj Mahal – although I was horrified to see that it had graffiti scratched all over it, and that the building is slowly being eaten away by acid rain giving the beautiful white marble a pitted surface. In contrast to that I also remember a rat scurrying out my bathroom once but in spite of these sorts of incidents we were really treated like kings wherever we went. There were extremes too like seeing young beggars with no legs in the streets in the morning and then being invited to the British Embassy for gin and tonics in the afternoon.

I learned a lot of my hockey on that tour and I've always been very appreciative of what the Indians have done for me. I found one restaurant where I requested, and was given, the hottest curry they had. I couldn't begin to eat it but I think that Bernie Cotton actually ordered a second one! Another funny story was when we hired a first-class bus to take us from one city to another and it turned out to be no more than a rickety old banger and probably one of the first buses ever built. It had no more than a piece of hardboard for a seat, and when we complained that we had ordered a first-class bus, they took the vehicle round the back and screwed another piece of hardboard down on to the existing one and brought it back! This rigmarole continued and finally we were given cushions to put down and we decided that we had to leave or we would never get out of the place. We set off and within ten minutes I fell asleep, and when we were stopped about three hours later I awoke to discover the most horrific sunburn on the side of my arm which had been hanging out of the window.

The police had chased behind us and brought the coach to a halt because apparently there was a cyclone that had just hit the city we were travelling to for our next match. Eventually the government ordered a plane to be chartered to take us back in reasonable safety, and we heard later that the city had been totally destroyed.

The stadium we played in at Nagpur was an enormous concrete structure and looked more like a Roman amphitheatre than anything else. The pitch didn't have a blade of grass on it, but there were still women walking along with watering cans watering the pitch. There was also the biggest steam roller I've ever seen – being pulled by an army of Indian labourers since they didn't have any fuel to run it! It was an unforgettable sight to see the women with their watering cans and the men straining in front with their roller on this bone-dry pitch!

SOVIET UNION

I do think our view of Eastern bloc countries tends to be heavily influenced by propaganda and supposition, and I'm not sure what's true and what isn't. I do know, however, that in the 1979 European club championships the Russian side, to a man, was the same as the national team. The teams they play for are called 'Dynamo' teams which allegedly means that they are something to do with the KGB. I'm never quite sure.

The Russians were never much of a force until the 1970s, and when the Games went to Moscow in 1980 a lot of time and resources were put into developing their hockey system. Internationally respected coaches were invited to the Soviet Union to try and expand the game. Considering that they had a limited club system they quickly achieved results, based primarily on their impressive physical strength and level of fitness. You certainly couldn't say that they have flair but they have always been effective at creating a physical barrier which is difficult for their opponents to penetrate. It's not very often that they've scored more than two goals in a match.

I gather from talking to some the Soviet players that the national sides train in institutions, and that people training for all different sports do their morning fitness training together, so that they utilise the flexibility of each sport and make it work for the others. In the afternoon they specialise in their own particular sports. I believe that the rewards for playing

116

international hockey are not bad and that none of them work whilst they are preparing for tournaments. Their needs are well looked after, but obviously the biggest perk for them is having the opportunity to travel the world. It was made public knowledge in the 1988 Olympics that Russian athletes would be financially rewarded for winning medals and I don't doubt that this has happened in the hockey world at European and World Cup level. But the Soviets have never been a serious threat, and have seldom got in amongst the medals at major tournaments.

I remember going to Moscow for the European Cup in 1987, where we stayed in a hotel that is reputedly the largest in the world. There seemed to be thousands of corridors and miles of rooms, and every doorway and corridor looked identical! The food was simply awful and because it was made at a specific time for so many people it was invariably cold. Everyone raved about the butter though – rumoured to be part of the EEC surplus that had been almost given away to Russia.

The dourness of Moscow struck me and even Red Square lacked the wonderful aura and atmosphere that there is when you go past the Houses of Parliament or Buckingham Palace for example. We didn't go out much, though, and in fairness I'm sure that we didn't see all that we should have.

HONG KONG AND SINGAPORE

I've played in Hong Kong and Singapore many times because they are convenient stopping-off places when we go to tournaments in Australia or the Far East. Like any sport over there, hockey in Hong Kong and Singapore is very exclusive and run along colonial lines. There's no real competition there, since there's not really anyone to play against. However I'd love to go back as a tourist rather than a hockey player – both Hong Kong and Singapore are visual feasts and I'd like to like to be able to let my hair down without the inevitable pre-match tension I usually experience in both places.

SPAIN

Spain has never really made a lasting impression on me, although it is very noticeable that hockey still carries a very rigid social status and is strictly a game for the middle and upper classes. I strongly disagree with this and think that it's not good for the game. The magnificent Polo Club in Barcelona has been the venue for some fantastic times, but I do wish that hockey could be opened out to the less privileged and not be quite as exclusive.

FRANCE AND ITALY

Hockey is trying very hard in these two countries to establish itself, and there has been a lot of money poured into the game to improve standards. Italy have brought in Dutch and German coaches and it does look unusual when you see a Pakistani playing in their club teams! The French have probably been more successful in their efforts, but it's my recollection of the Italians at tournaments that springs to mind. At the European Championships at Lille in France one year the Italians captivated everyone with their quite incredible clothes and debonair appearance! They were without doubt the 'posiest' bunch of sportsmen I'd ever seen! All their tracksuits, bags and stickbags were individually embroidered and their clothes all had designer labels. All their equipment was brand new and they made most professional tennis players look like paupers. It was unfortunate that they weren't very good hockey players!

ARGENTINA

I took part in my first major tournament, the World Cup, in Beunos Aires, which was held three months after the football

World Cup in 1978. There were several scares concerning terrorist threats, and we would travel in the coach with personal bodyguards, two police cars riding either side, motorcyclists driving on to stop traffic and red lights flashing. One incident that was a bit alarming at the time occurred when I walked out of the hotel one day to go and sit in a park to relax. A member of the public approached me for my autograph and put his hand in his jacket to get out the pen and paper. Suddenly a bodyguard went for him and in seconds had him in a tight grip before he had any idea as to what was going on. Of course it was all a misunderstanding and we managed to resolve the matter amicably but it gave me fright at the time. I was wandering back to the hotel musing over what an over-reaction it had been when, just as I got within sight of the railway station, three bombs went off in it. I could actually see the glass and doors flying and then heard the massive boom as they exploded.

The Argentinian captain, Marcelo Garraffo, who is such an internationally respected player, made his debut at the tournament. Although he plays in the midfield now, he was centre-forward then and I can remember saving three penalty strokes he took against me. Argentina are another team who have promised much but have somehow never quite fulfilled their potential.

MIDDLE EAST

I have toured a few countries in the Middle East, notably Oman and Kuwait. The reason for going there is that the Arabs like to be entertained and sport is a method of doing this. There is also a strong Pakistani workforce in the Arab states which promotes hockey. We went to play there because our Association was offered money and it was enough to cover training weekends to prepare the squad right up until the next Champions' Trophy so it could hardly be turned down.

The opulence was staggering and the hotel we stayed in was absolutely sparkling and consisted of nothing but the best.

Because of an International Football Association ruling stating that all internationals had to be played on grass, two months before we went out they tore up the artificial surface in the stadium and put grass down. The other pitch was rolled up outside when we arrived. Conditions were very hot, it was a bumpy surface and we came fourth out of four in the first tournament, and then first in the second one.

I can't see the Arab States ever having their own indigenous hockey system, since most hockey players there are immigrants. Hockey, like many other sports, is taken over there simply to entertain the wealthy and remains an exhibition for the affluent.

I've only been able to give here a skeleton impression of the countries I've travelled in – if space permitted many would deserve a chapter in their own right. Playing hockey around the world for 12 years may have been exhausting, but nothing could have been more rewarding. Despite the occasional traumas of foreign travel, I have some terrifically fond memories of countries and players across the world.

8
THE OLYMPIC CHALLENGE

The hockey team for the Olympic Games is selected as it would be for any other tournament, but it is not selected to represent the Great Britain Hockey Board or the constituent associations. It is chosen to represent the British Olympic Association and becomes part of the British Olympic team. Each hockey player then becomes every much a part of the British team as does an athlete, a boxer or a swimmer.

After selection, one of the first things Olympic teams have to do is sort out their kit. The team uniform is all pre-determined and every member of the team is handed the same items. Our first set of hockey shirts for Seoul were a disaster and the smallest size was a 56-inch chest, which needless to say we weren't entirely happy with! The next set were a better fit but one of the chaps who had one of the 56-size shirts said that when it came back from the wash it had shrunk to a 32! I know lots of people see the uniformity of the kit as a threat to their individuality, but I think it's most important. The British team uniform gives a lasting impression, and helps to tell the world how proud we are of our team.

Since the awful disasters that have befallen previous Games, security matters are treated extremely seriously. The security starts long before you even arrive at the airport. There are innumerable forms to be filled in, some for team or BOA publicity but a lot of them presumably for painstaking cross-checking and security examination. The restrictions continue when you get to the airport. All the baggage is marked as Olympic property and from that moment onwards the x-rays, metal detector tests and scannings start. It doesn't only happen to the suitcases and kit, but to all the athletes – several times over! In my case, being a goalkeeper, I carry an enormous amount of luggage, and I always have to perform miracles to get the stuff closed. Two sets of pads and two sets of kickers require a certain amount of magician's art to get into a case designed for one set of each! There is nothing more disheartening than when a security man stands in front of you and demands that it is all opened up! It's a real pain at the time, but it's all being done in the interests of the athletes' safety.

My feelings upon arrival at the Olympic village in 1984 and 1988 were completely different. In 1984 I had been catapulted suddenly into the whole Olympic scenario and was quite swept away with the excitement of it all, whereas in 1988 I was properly prepared and went with a job to do, unfazed by all the razzamatazz.

Superficially, however, Los Angeles and Seoul were fairly similar. The stringent security was the same with 15-foot high barbed wire all around the perimeter, in double rows with a gap in between that was patrolled by dogs. From there of course the rigmarole of checking in and out of the village begins. The identity tags that every athlete, official and media person are issued with to wear round their neck, serve as an essential passport to wherever you are permitted to go.

In Los Angeles there were two villages set up at either university (we stayed at UCLA), but in Seoul there was a purpose-built village. UCLA was an established campus and we were merely a new set of students replacing those that were on vacation. It was a most relaxing atmosphere and accommodation was log cabin-style, the restaurants were well organised and we quickly settled in. There was an enormous array of facilities available – an Olympic-size swimming pool, leisure centre, and even a crew of qualified masseurs to see to our needs, as well as a Vidal Sassoon hairdressers where you could have your hair cut free of charge! The accommodation was a little cramped, however, because there were six beds pushed into a space for two.

Because I'm not really a person who enjoys high rise buildings and thousands of people everywhere, I found the conditions at Seoul a little claustrophobic at times. There were eight team members per apartment and the five men in the management shared a third. There were three double rooms and two singles per apartment, with the two goalkeepers each having the luxury of a single room. This was not only because of all the extra space our equipment takes up but also because after a few days it begins to get very smelly and unpleasant! Our room allocations were always decided by the management who determined who got on with who, or in some cases who would be a bad influence on someone else! For example, Sean Kerly and Steve Batchelor wouldn't be allowed to share a room because they were very good pals off the pitch and would probably stay up far too late! There is also a certain amount of team development that has to be done and those younger players in the squad who haven't been away from home often need to be with somebody who can help them through it. Others are affected differently by tournament play and you can't have an abrasive character sharing with a guy who is very introverted. David Faulkner and Jon Potter were sharing, as were Sam Martin and Richard Leman, Richard Dodds and Sean Kerly, Steve Batchelor and Russell Garcia, Paul Barber and Kulbeir Bhaura, Jimmy Kirkwood and Martyn Grimley and Robert Clift and Imran Sherwani. It's most important for team morale that the pairings work well.

Although the facilities in the athletes' village were incredible by normal standards, the Koreans couldn't actually cope with the influx of people. When we first saw the third floor with all its beautiful furnishings and five snooker tables we couldn't help marvelling, until we realised that with the amount of athletes present it would be just about impossible to ever get a game. There was another room with 30 computer games but again, it was a totally inadequate number for the thousands of individuals it was supposed to cater for. The Koreans worked very hard to make all the facilities as agreeable as possible and attempted to overcome all the problems encountered, but too often they were defeated by numbers. Queuing became very much a way of life in the Olympic village.

In Seoul we soon got to know all the athletes in the blocks closest to us, and it wasn't long before all the other athletes had draped flags over their balconies to make sure everyone knew which country they were from! We became very friendly with the Canadians directly opposite, and we also had several African nations near us. It was quite funny because some of the Kenyan hockey team live in England and I knew them well.

You never know who you'll bump into the Olympics. Lots of people had bought funny sunglasses with the Olympic rings on them, and when I looked more closely on one occasion I realised that it was Captain Mark Phillips wearing a pair! It's not the popular image of him but I do think it emphasises how competitors can relax and I found it disappointing that the likes of Steve Cram and Daley Thompson chose not to stay in the village. On the two nights I went out to dinner at a hotel I was dismayed to see them enjoying the luxuries of one of the top hotels. They may have felt that staying at the Olympic village would affect their chances of a medal and no doubt the autograph-hunters would have frustrated them, but it was a lovely surprise to see Chris Evert, Stefan Edberg and Steffi Graf walking around the village. It made Steve Batchelor's day when Mecir, the eventual tennis gold medallist, collected his tray of food and came to sit down next to him. That's what the Olympics is all about.

I think that message came over very strongly. It was the World Games and everyone was prepared to sit down and live side by side. Whoever would have thought that you could see, as I did, two athletes sitting next to one another, one with Iran on his tracksuit, and the other with Iraq. Politics and conflicts were completely forgotten. There was one lovely story about the British rower, Steve Redgrave, who was having enormous problems with his boat until the Russians' engineer stepped in to help. He mended it to perfection and it is well known that Steve and Andy Holmes went on to win the gold medal. But as Steve pointed out afterwards, he needn't have done that for the British and by doing so he more or less made sure that the Soviet's main rivals had a boat in good condition.

It was easy to get into a 'face spotting' situation by parking yourself in a quiet corner and just observing all the famous athletes going by. Russell Garcia, in his first Olympics at Seoul, used to be entranced by the celebrities passing him. One day Robert Clift and Jon Potter positioned themselves around a corner when they knew he would be coming past and as he did so they said: 'Ooh, look, there's Russell Garcia!'

Russell wasn't the only one who got teased. Martyn Grimley was always amazingly particular about his hairstyle and before he went into the cafeteria he would spend ages making sure that not a hair was out of place!. We did wonder who he was trying to impress!

After a while you can get almost blasé about sitting next to millionaire sports personalities. What is very difficult for people to comprehend is that hockey continues throughout the Games and therefore it's almost impossible to socialise at any length with the other athletes you may strike up a friendship with. We saw Fatima Whitbread a lot because she used to come up and use our video, but apart from that sort of isolated incident, you tend to stick in your own group and maintain your identity – which after all is very important when you're performing in team events.

I'll never forget the Bulgarian and Soviet gymnasts. The girls really are tiny and because they are so young they were frog-marched about by their coaches or minders. It was interesting to see how they responded to the atmosphere of the Olympics. However frosty they might appear on TV, the gymnasts are in reality just normal, excited little girls, in awe of what is going on around them. As for the men, I've always been intrigued by the size of their bulging muscles, but when you actually stand alongside them you realise that they are actually much less than six foot tall but those muscles aren't so big after all! Of course it's all relative, and in relation to their size their muscles are impressive.

One of the little Bulgarian girls was obviously addicted to a particular chocolate drink that was available in the cafeteria which you had to pour into boiling water. It was supposedly forbidden to take any food out with you but every meal-time she would surreptitiously sneak about half a dozen in to her pocket, and slip away with them! Likewise our guys took to the ice cream which in fact was so delicious it became an instant success with all the teams. Tracksuits or hoods would suddenly assume all sorts of shapes and jerseys would cover up several cartons of ice cream being smuggled out for a later feast!

I was also intrigued by the women dressed up in brightly coloured clothes who would stand outside the dining room. It took us about six days to realise that they were security guards and were all highly trained and armed! Most of them were very good looking and little did we know that they were perfectly capable of confronting anyone they suspected of being an aggressor. They checked our identities scrupulously just to ensure that we were in fact going in to have a meal.

Outside the Olympic village there were two or three venues within walking range, but I must confess that I was so concerned about the hockey that I never managed to get to them. Some of our lads would often go over and watch the tennis, swimming or gymnastics which were ten minutes away. The only stadium I went to was the main athletics stadium, where I watched 'Flo Jo' setting two world records and Daley Thompson breaking a pole in the pole vault! I think I also saw a women's world record in the long jump, but what most people don't realise is how vast the stadium is and that because everything is so far away all you see is a mere speck in the distance followed by a huge roar from the crowd. I found I couldn't really relate to athletics and found it all rather disjointed over a period of three or four hours.

It was interesting to hear all the reactions from the various competitors about their stadiums. Adrian Moorhouse came back and described the Olympic swimming pool as 'good' and 'fast!' I thought for a bit that he was pulling my leg but after he explained I understood far more about the technicalities of an Olympic pool. Conditions can be affected by all sorts of things from water temperature to the type of paint on the bottom of the pool. Athletes said that it was a 'fast' track and generally, opinions were that the purpose-built facilities were some of the best ever seen.

The Songnam hockey stadium seated more than 25,000 spectators and was built for the Asian Games. Outside the main stadium was a smaller practice pitch, but I think that most clubs in the British Isles would have been more than happy to own the 'practice' pitch! The two pitches were both constructed of different artificial surfaces and we had to play three pool matches on the outside pitch whereas all the other sides had two. Happily the surfaces didn't make any difference although the long or short pile, amount of watering, and hardness can make a difference. It's something that should be carefully monitored in future and home teams should be prevented from giving themselves any unfair advantage.

Facilities in the main stadium were absolutely fabulous, with immaculate changing rooms, superb pitch, great spectator facilities and enormous scoreboards. To get to the stadium each time we had our own coach and driver, plus personal protection agent, liaison man and an interpreter. As soon as the coach left the village it automatically picked up one or two policemen on motor bikes, and at times we had a police car. The effect these officials had was amazing! A blink of a light or a siren, and traffic lights on red would turn to green, traffic jams parted like the Red Sea and journeys became very easy.

I used to daydream away the journey to the Songnam Stadium. Leaving the city we would pass an agricultural area and then a couple of colleges and a university, which we used for practice areas before the Games began. It was whilst practising that we realised that the Koreans didn't have a hockey club system at all. They had created a hockey system especially for the Olympics, and the educational facilities were used to find and coach players. And I think that again this shows how much prestige the Koreans attached to hosting the Olympics and performing well in them. This professional approach was reflected in both their hockey teams winning the Asian Games in 1986.

Any Korean who had the potential to become an Olympian was immediately relieved of their job, their pay was continued and provision was made for their housing and food. I understand that anyone who won a gold medal was paid a lump sum instantly and paid a pension for life. The rewards obviously diminished proportionately according to the type of medal won. The wonderful facilities all over the city meant that the Koreans had been able to train daily in the best possible circumstances for the past few years.

I think their approach shows what an industrious and ambitious nation the Koreans are. Cost, time and effort proved to be no object to them and their patience and politeness won them warm praise from everyone. It's no wonder, if rumours are to be believed, that the Japanese are becoming wary of their success and the positive advances that the Koreans have made in their economy. The single-mindedness and energy of the Koreans will almost certainly result in a highly successful future. The Koreans are a very proud nation and whether that is as a result of past conflicts in their country or something that has developed recently I don't know. They have made themselves into a major sporting and financial influence in the East, and it's not surprising that success is so important to them.

That is why I admire their hockey players. Because there is no club set-up they all have to learn their hockey from the same source and then play each other again and again and again to improve. The only route to prosperity in the international arena is through tournament play, and because the financial support is forthcoming they are able to stage a lot of them. And their progress has been phenomenal.

The strides thay have made was highlighted by their ladies' team winning the silver medal. They were absolutely super athletes and I think they were quite capable of winning the gold medal. The discrepancy between the different women's teams in athleticism was incredible and I would single it out as the major difference between the British women and their Korean counterparts. One must bear in mind though that the Korean women were paid to train and the British girls were genuine amateurs who took time off work and all had careers. It will be interesting to see whether they can maintain the level of success that they have achieved.

In the week we spent in Seoul before the Games started, we trained and played practice matches, including one against Australia. Obviously we wanted to test ourselves against top class opposition and because they weren't in our group we felt confident about playing them without giving away too many trade secrets. We played three sessions, of which I played in two, and from the way I performed I felt extremely confident at the outset that I would be in good form for the tournament. Whilst the third session was in progress Roger Self, our manager, sneaked alongside me. He had been missing up until this stage and I wondered what what he was going to tell me. He leant over and whispered: 'I've got some good news for you.' I was bursting to know what he was going to say! He eventually continued: 'You've been chosen to carry the British flag in the Opening Ceremony – more about it later! And not a word to anybody, an announcement will be made! He then dashed off.

I couldn't believed it, and it was awful to have to keep it to myself. So there I was at the back of the stand, grinning like a Cheshire cat – everyone who was walking past must have wondered what on earth I was looking so smug for! At the end of the game we had a little presentation from the Mayor of Songnam who, for some reason, gave us all a pair of ski gloves! Then Roger pulled the team together, and with a great flourish announced that I had been elected to carry the flag. Naturally there was a fair amount of leg pulling, and continuing the theme of the well-known athletes who said they wouldn't be attending the Opening Ceremony, most of our chaps started to say that they weren't sure if they'd be going either!

It was a wonderful moment for hockey and Roger explained to me later what the procedure had been. All team managers meet and nominate a candidate and once the CVs are read out, a shortlist is made up. The managers all vote and then a final list of four is made and there is a further round of voting before the successful person is chosen. I felt that it was recognition for hockey, that hockey would be walking out in front and saying: 'Look out, here we are and we're going to stay out in front!'

I 'phoned home as soon as I could but because of the time difference and the delay in getting back from the hockey stadium and the press conference, it meant that people in England already knew. Immediately one television company organised a live link-up with Julie, and I phoned my mother. They both said how immensely proud they felt. The telegrams piled up and my bedroom walls were adorned with telegrams and cards from the Minister of Sport, club members, the BOA, Hockey Association and even my bank manager!

People would keep asking me if I was nervous about carrying the flag but I wasn't at all. One of the BOA officials tried to coach in the best method of carrying it and I soon felt confident about what I was expected to do. I knew I had to salute the President of Korea but nobody had told me anything about the swearing of the Olympic oath!

All the athletes were bussed to the warm-up stadium which was right next door to the main Olympic athletics one. The Korean women dressed in traditional fashion who were carrying the team names were all around, and we were instructed to line up behind them. As we were about to start a whole lot of camera crews arrived to interview me but it wasn't long before we were off! The minute I walked proudly into the Stadium I was hit by the incredible atmosphere, and felt another huge swell of pride. I felt proud to be British and even more proud to be leading our team in.

It was quite amusing when we were walking because behind me someone was shouting 'slow down, slow down' and ahead of me the Korean girl was telling me to hurry up! I struck a happy medium in the end. During the ceremony all the flag bearers are called over to a spot to take the oath and say the Olympic prayer. I was caught completely off my guard not having been warned, but managed to catch up with the others when I realised what was happening! There were several big chaps who had the strength to hold their flag with one arm and I tried to do likewise, little realising at the time just what a painful ordeal that would be! One little African chap was holding his flag up high but he too was battling and every so often his flag would go all over the show and bump into mine and all those near him. Try as we might it became very difficult to keep them still and I think anyone watching must have wondered what was happening!

As I walked out of the arena with the flag, the BBC and ITV crews conducted some interviews and I was caught up with them for about twenty minutes after everyone had left. I have to admit that as I stood there with the flag in my hands, I thought that if there is a souvenir then this has got to be it! The flag and the pole was approximately eight foot long, so I unscrewed it, wrapped it all up into a bundle and went back towards the coaches to go back to the village. On the way to the car park the Koreans kept stopping me and requesting that I return the flag but I was determined not to and carried on walking! I'd have paid them for it and it was one of the rare occasions in my life that I have stolen anything.

It stayed in my room throughout the Games, and now stands proudly in my house. I'm still waiting for the bill from Korea! When we had the celebration match at Luton at the end of November to mark our triumph, because I had retired I was asked to carry the flag in at the beginning of the evening. It was fantastic to see nearly 9,000 spectators at a hockey match on a cold, wintry Wednesday night and I experienced the same warm feelings of pride when I entered Luton as I had on that Saturday afternoon in Seoul.

One has to try and live life in the Olympics by all the moral ethics that one would like to uphold. Unfortunately the rewards are sometimes so high and the promises of fame and fortune so lavish that people tend to search for unfair means of attaining these goals. All sorts of methods of cheating are resorted to whether it be sabres with artificial tips or drugs that build stronger muscles or help to reduce weight. You never hear about drug abuse in hockey, but I suppose you never know if a particularly strong athlete has taken drugs to enhance his or her performance. I hope not, because the whole emphasis at the Olympics is on the spirit and that spirit doesn't involve cheating. I think drug abuse should be stamped out and heavily punished by the authorities. The problem arises of how not to penalise athletes who have taken medication for a genuine reason such as a headache or cold but who are, unfortunately, transgressing the law. There was one American athlete who was an asthmatic and had been taking a drug for 12 years, but was still stripped of his gold medal. Rumours begin to fly around when there is an incident, and after the Ben Johnson affair, people were quick to start pointing accusing fingers. But I think that one has to very sceptical over some of the incredible feats achieved by some of the athletes. As far as I'm concerned punishment should be nothing less than a life ban. The only way the general public will have any confidence in the performances of sportsmen is by those involved taking a forthright stand on the issue.

The Olympic motto – stronger, higher, faster – has been the key element in both closing ceremonies that I've been to. As an athlete you don't really see the spectacle of what's going on in the stadium because you're right down there in the midst of it all and in fact, the athletes are the spectacle. You experience a marvellous atmosphere but it's completely different to the opening ceremony. It's almost like a drunken fervour, with everyone relaxed, happy and laughing. On both occasions when the words stronger, higher and faster were spoken, I thought about how much had been achieved and how much a part of the world community I was. I was privileged to have realised my dreams in that fantastic environment, and I felt able to leave completely contented. I felt that I would never need anything from sport again. Seoul was my finale and nothing could have bettered it.

9
THE PLAYERS AND THE PLAYING

There have been so many players and memorable moments in my career that I had to think for a long time before I could recall those who have either made a significant contribution to my own development or who have featured in unforgettable incidents. Whoever I've named, I've done so for a specific reason and it certainly hasn't been my intention to upset anybody. Any revelations, therefore, are merely an insight into a particular phase or underlying theme.

The first two people I'd like to mention are two former Indian internationals and Olympians, who played for Bourneville club in Birmingham when I was a young lad and eager to learn all I could about the game. They were called Darchand and Gurjit and both played for Worcestershire. I got to know them when I was selected to play in the odd representative game, which often meant that I would either play with or against them. They made a lasting impression on me for several reasons. Darchand had the most amazing stickwork and there was no player in English hockey at the time who could possibly match his skills. He could control the ball so well that it seemed as though it was stuck to his stick and he would weave his way effortlessly round defenders.

His ability to mesmerise the opposition was incredible, but what also impressed me greatly was his character and attitude to sport. Darchand really taught me about dedication and he was adamant that if you wanted to achieve anything you had to practise, practise and practise. I think he was as much my Bobby Moore or Gary Lineker as the footballers were or are today and I could happily sit, stand, watch and listen to him for hours. I was totally in awe of him. His example showed me how important it is for the players of today to be a positive influence on youth and to be fully aware of the responsibilities that international success carries. His impeccable behaviour as a sportsman was something I have never forgotten and I tried throughout my career to adhere to his principles.

I only ever saw him get angry once and that was in a game when a striker was giving me a torrid time and kept knocking me down. Darchand was furious and I remember that for the next ten minutes, whenever he got the ball, he would make straight for this player and torment him by playing the ball in and out of his legs to make a complete fool of him! He neither spoke nor touched him until he had done this numerous times, then he said: 'Now you play the game properly!'

Gurjit was a fine 'old' gentleman. Old because he was probably about forty when I was in my teens and that seemed very old! He taught me just what a hockey stick and ball could do. He could make a ball swerve to the left or the right, he could make it dip or rise and he could make it spin on the surface. In my early days he would hit to me and tell me what the ball was going to do and how he was going to do it. In time I got the hang of it and got a bit cocky, and then he would quickly bring me down to size by consistently beating me by hitting it between my legs! He did it by getting me to go the right way but his skill in getting the ball to deviate would always beat me. He taught me the necessity of being humble and accepting that no person is bigger than the sport that they're participating in.

I know that I've missed out hundreds of people who have made an impression on me, people like Mark Rendall who was a real clown and also numerous club players I've come across. Those of particular note are Paul Schveelik, who is now European controller for the World Circuit Tennis in Paris and was once an England tennis player as was Steve Long, another character. Their approach to sport at the time was that it was to be keenly contested but it wasn't to interfere with life too much, and training was certainly never allowed to stop you enjoying yourself! The first port of call after a match was always the bar, and I remember at one of my first international tournaments in Amsterdam we beat West Germany for the first time in 20 years. The scenes in the bar had to be seen to be believed and the fact that there was an international the next day was totally irrelevant!

That would be quite unacceptable nowadays – although of course there have to be celebrations, there are right and wrong times to let your hair down! I think that was a reason why England and GB were never world beaters, because they were never unified in thought or objective and everyone did his own thing. The German side of 1972, that were coming to the end of a hugely successful era, showed me what dedication and commitment are all about. I can recall that Steve Long, who played on the left wing, would often have a gin and tonic before he went out on the pitch just to steady his nerves!

I certainly used to get irritated with their attitude and I used to shout at a lot of players, particularly the defence, if I felt that they weren't pulling out all the stops and working hard enough, especially after a late night! I lost my temper a lot of times and in the World Cup in 1978 once again I had a go at them. We were facing our eighth penalty corner against West Germany and I think that they decided that they'd had enough of this young upstart! Dave Whitaker turned round to me and told me in no uncertain terms to 'shut up!' I think I've mellowed a bit since then and although right up until the 1988 Olympics I continued to bellow, particularly at Steve Batchelor, I learned to try not to upset players. If I ever felt that I had shouted out of turn I would apologise afterwards and say I felt that perhaps it had been unnecessary.

During that era I remember two players in particular. One was my predecessor Peter Mills who was a giant of a man and who had a habit of creating a horizontal barrier. One story of his reign concerned a ten-mile training run that they had all been sent out on. After three hours when he hadn't returned they went out and found him enjoying himself on a pub crawl! I used to watch him when I was aspiring to greater things and recall how boring I thought he made the position look. I felt he didn't add any excitement or bubble to the game and I decided that if ever took over from him then I would make goalkeeping fun.

I think my image was reinforced by a Spanish goalkeeper called Carrera who was completely the opposite. He embodied all the qualities of Latin-blooded sportsmen and was pure entertainment. He was totally unorthodox, could never be relied upon to do anything twice, would make brilliant saves and let the simplest of goals in! I remember him playing once in Barcelona and a German came in the circle and unleashed a fierce drive which headed for the top corner of the net. Carrera need only have dived and palmed the ball away with his hand but no! As the shot came in, he took off into the air and with a spectacular overhead scissors kick cleared the ball from just underneath his crossbar over the sideline!

Naturally the crowd were enthralled and when we were in the bar afterwards I mentioned it to him and asked him how he did it. He grinned and replied: 'If you think you can, you can!' In an exhibition match in Holland several years later, a shot came in at me that took a wicked deflection and was flying into the roof of the net. And in that split second I made the decision to emulate Carrera and flipped up and, in identical fashion, cleared the ball over the halfway line! A young boy came up to me after the game and asked me how I did it and because I didn't have the nerve to pretend I had practised it I said: 'Somebody once told me that if you think you can, you can!' I always tried to carry that philosophy through especially in the exhibition games.

The players I'd like to mention now are some who impressed me not only as hockey players and sportsmen but also because we became friends. We shared international sporting experiences not only on the pitch but off it as well. Ajit Pal was a legendary Indian centre-half who had a marvellous reign in the 1970s. He was a very tall man and it goes without saying that he had all the magical skills that most Asians seem to possess. But the reason I remember him was a particular tournament that we played in in New Delhi – his home city. He was the local hero and during the final they were all over us. We simply didn't have an answer to the Indians, and although the score was 0–0 at half time we literally hadn't managed to break into their half. Out of our squad of 16, five had dysentery and Paul Barber played the game with a cork lodged in a rather crucial position! John Hurst watched the match from a toilet which was situated conveniently near the pitch! Eventually, Steve Long picked up the ball on the halfway line and dribbled his way into their half. Because so many of the opposition were committed to attacking he was able to force his way into the circle and sent a rocket of a shot in the goal, only for the umpire to disallow it for offside! On their fifth penalty stroke (I had already saved four!) the striker sent me the wrong way, only for the ball to hit the crossbar. The action had begun.

The most memorable incident occurred when our centre-forward Bal Saini, a Kenyan Asian with British nationality, was dribbling the ball. As he went past Ajit Pal his stick accidentally caught him and opened up a nasty gash above Ajit's eye. It was the signal for the crowd to react and, incensed that their hero had been felled, they erupted in uproar. As he lay on the ground the unrest grew and more and more missiles were hurled on to the pitch by the 12,000-strong crowd. The police tried to halt it but it didn't stop and when Ajit Pal had to leave to have several stitches inserted, we were the targets for seats, bits of the stands and even metal piping.

138

We began to get a bit frightened and all the England players moved into a huddle in the middle of the pitch. Behind the bench was the VIP area where all the high-ranking officials were sitting. There were little tables in front of each chair with pots of tea on them, and when we looked up towards this area we saw all the officials starting to hurl tables, chairs, cups and saucers on to the pitch! After we had stood for about 20 minutes Ajit came back with stitches in his head and made an announcement over the public address system. He said that the injury had been an accident, that he had accepted the apology and please could the game continue! With that the crowd returned to their seats, the soldiers rushed on to clear the debris and the game carried on!

There was one funny incident in India on that tour that I shall never forget, which occurred when we went to a large colonial-style house to rest for a few days. Most of the team used the time to recover from the debilitating effects of amoebic dysentery and enjoy the rather luxurious lifestyle at this splendid home. The Indian who looked after us claimed he was of Scottish descent and wore a kilt all the time! But he spoke in broken English and looked quite a sight in this kilt. On one occasion we were sitting down drinking beer on the verandah while he was voicing his opinions on several matters. He got more and more worked up and then suddenly reached into his kilt and pulled out a revolver and fired a shot in to the roof! We all leapt up and gazed in amazement at the hole in the roof until he told us all not to worry and we sat down again somewhat warily. It wasn't ten minutes later that he did the same thing again but by this time we were getting used to him! As he got drunker and drunker we started to wind him up and he entertained us all evening blasting away with his revolver!

We were staying in colonial-type cottages away from the main building, where John Hurst and I were sharing one half of an apartment and Dave Whitaker and Paul Barber the other. One of the main talking points of the evening had been creepy crawlies and it had emerged that Paul was terrified of them! Of course an evening of drinking beer combined with that knowledge gave me all the incentive I needed. We all switched our lights off, and having told John what I was going to do, got out of bed and stealthily crawled on my hands and knees through to Paul and Dave's room. I found my way over to Paul's bed and as the Barber snore was just starting I knew he was asleep! I moved my hand up underneath the mosquito netting and began to simulate a spider with my fingers slowly crawling all over him. You could tell by the shudder of the bed that he had sat bold upright and was sitting there terrified! Eventually I got to his foot and gave a good 'bite' at which point Paul leapt out of bed – all 6′ 2″ and 13 stone of him, and brought all the netting down in a bundle! We laughed for ages after that and although he threatened to decapitate me he did at least see the funny side!

It was during the course of that evening that John took ill with amoebic dysentery and woke me up by crying out constantly in the night. At first I though he was messing around and threw all manner of things at him including a hockey boot which caught him across his face. When he didn't wake up with that I realised that something was wrong. He had lapsed into a coma and we had to get emergency treatment and call out doctors for him. I'm happy to say that he made a full recovery but that was one of the hazards of travelling to India.

It was at the 1978 World Cup in Buenos Aires that I first met Michael Peter who was the West German sweeper and one of the world's greatest players at the time. All the teams had been subject to stringent security because of threats by terrorist groups, and we all had personal security guards which became a bit tiresome after a while. Michael and I decided to go out one evening once the tournament had finished, but we didn't want to take bodyguards because we wanted to see the town ourselves and do our own thing without anyone constantly following us. The only way we could get out without attracting the attention of the guards was to climb down the balconies of the hotel from the outside. We didn't think much about it, and scrambled our way down seven floors with absolutely no regard for our safety or the drop below us! Once in the city we had a marvellous time, in and out it bars and seeing the nightlife for ourselves. Although he was nearing the end of his career we remained good friends. I admired all he had done and his identified with his sentiments about playing in the Olympics. I saw him as one of the sport's real gentlemen, and I know that he was enormously respected for both his extraordinary ability and his charming personality.

Another superb sportsman was the German left-winger of that era, Peter Trump, who many people believed bore an uncanny resemblance to me. I remember watching him at Lord's once and he was magnificent. I heard that he contracted hepatitis which he never really got over and which effectively ruined his sporting career. Wolfgang Strodter, the infamous penalty corner striker, was also in the German side at this time and was another man for whom I had great respect.

It was the Germans' professional approach to the game that I particularly admired. Michael Peter helped me mould certain ideas on how to improve English hockey, and our long chats strengthened my convictions about what we should be doing in the game and how we could benefit from the German approach.

Martin Sikking, the Dutch goalkeeper, was one player who impressed me at the start of my international career. He was the only goalkeeper I've ever seen who held his stick in his left hand and who invariably cleared the ball, flicked it or stopped it with his stick on the reverse. That was his individuality. He was a quiet and unassuming chap but very definite in his objectives and how he played the game. What rubbed off on me was his total conviction about believing in yourself. I think he probably continued playing when he was past his best. He had suffered numerous knee problems but this isn't unusual because most goalkeepers tend to get those sort of injuries or rheumatism in the joints from all the knocks and twisting. Dutch goalkeepers would never warm up in their pads, but would wear their tracksuit and then run around and stretch until they felt warm before putting on all their padding and kickers. Both of his knees were a mess and I know he had quite a few operations. I remember him warming up for a game once and all you could hear was this incredible clicking noise. It took me quite some time to work out what this strange sound was and eventually I figured out that it was Martin's legs. They were in fact covered in multiple scars from operations – an awful sight. He told me that the longer he ran round and the longer he warmed the joints up, the less noise they would make. Seeing and hearing that, I came to the conclusion that that wasn't the price I wanted to pay and I would never let myself reach that desperate situation. Not only had he continued beyond his best, but he has also reached the limits of his physical capacity.

Paul Litjens, 'the Bull' or gentle giant of Dutch hockey, was another legend. He was undoubtedly one of the greatest corner strikers the game has ever known, and in 177 international appearances he scored an incredible 267 goals. He was enormously strong and a true gentleman who always loved playing and enjoying himself in the bar afterwards. He was determined to get as much from his hockey as he possibly could. I remember at the European Cup in 1979 Paul was being fêted as a superstar and Wrigley's were sponsoring him. He did a TV advertisement which was a bit of a fun thing, which involved the company setting up an enormous pair of scales at the ground. He sat on one side and they gave him as much chewing gum as fitted on the other side until the scales balanced. They piled box upon box and we all had a good laugh waiting for the scales to balance! Talking to him afterwards I asked him what he was going to do with so many boxes of chewing gum. He explained that he didn't get the chewing gum but the value of the gum that was in all the boxes, and besides which, he didn't really like chewing gum! In those days it must have come to a substantial amount in our amateur game.

The only time I ever saw Paul get angry was in the World Cup in Bombay in 1982/83. It was the first tournament where the Russian goalkeeper Pleshakov used the horizontal technique and blocked the penalty corner shot by lying down across the goalmouth. The Soviets had met with considerable success using this technique, and Pleshakov was employing the method with great effect against Paul. Shot after shot of Paul's was stopped and the 'keeper was taking fierce drives into his stomach, on his legs, arms and even to his head, and every time he would have to receive treatment, but the Dutch couldn't score. Paul was incensed and went up to the umpire and said that the Russians had a fullback on either post, and a goalkeeper lying down, and the only way he could hit the backboard with his shot was to hit Pleshakov. He told the umpire that in order to avoid hurting anyone he would place the ball in the middle of the goal just under the crossbar! That way, he insisted, he wouldn't harm anyone. At the very next corner, he did just that with unerring accuracy, straight into the roof of the net and nobody moved! But the umpire disallowed it for dangerous play. Despite Paul's animated protestations the umpire stood firm and of course was quite right to do so. He couldn't make any exceptions just because it was Paul Litjens. It was the end of his era because the goalkeeping style destroyed his ability to score and he lost his effectiveness. I thought it sad because Paul always enjoyed his hockey and although he wanted to score goals and be successful he wasn't prepared to knock chunks off goalkeepers in the process.

In Holland the Kruize family are legendry. Three brothers, Ties, Hans and Jan Hidde have won international hockey honours as has their sister. I would like to mention Ties who won the European superstars competition as well as 202 caps for Holland. He was a great sportsman but, in my opinion, another one who played on for too long. I think he kept going in the hope that he might achieve what he set out to do, but somehow he never quite did. One story about Ties concerns his benefit game to mark his retirement, a gesture not shown in British hockey. It was held between Europe and Australasia – in other words, Pakistan, India and Australia versus Germany, Britain, Holland and Spain. It was a fantastic atmosphere and Ties's contribution to hockey was recognized by the general public, his club, hockey lovers and the Dutch Association. He received an automatic golf buggy from his club as a thank you, and of course loads of other presents and donations. A vineyard in Germany even made a special wine and supplied it to everyone on the day as well as to Ties for as long as he wanted to drink it! The Dutch Board gave him 14 golfing lessons with Arnold Palmer in Florida, all expenses paid and over a three month period. Not bad for retiring I thought!

I always enjoyed my rivalry with Ties and it seemed to always surface at penalty strokes because he often took them. I know I saved quite a lot that he took but the highlight was at the 1984 Olympics when we had a tense match against the Dutch and I saved one from him. It resulted in our going through to the semi-finals and blew any hopes Holland had of qualifying clean away. I'll never forget the moment straight after the game when he came up to me, shook my hand and said: 'Well saved'. That meant an awful lot to me, and I have often wondered if I could ever have had the courage to do the same thing myself had I been faced with such a disappointment. Not content with that he sought me out and did exactly the same thing when we won the bronze medal.

I know he may be arrogant at times, but he has a definite aura about him which children find particularly appealing. Ties is a hero and he has the power to inspire tremendous enthusiasm amongst young players. One of the conditions that Ties insisted on for his benefit game was that every overseas player coached any young Dutch players who turned up. The whole of the morning before the match, therefore, was spent coaching children who derived enormous satisfaction from being personally helped by people like Terry Walsh, Hasan Sadar, David Bell, Heiner Dopp and Stefan Bloecher. I'm sure that he is financially secure now due to the game, but I don't believe that Ties has ever lost sight of what the sport is all about.

Moving onto some of the great Pakistanis, one of the first that comes to mind is Samiullah Khan, who played left-wing for Pakistan. He was one of the fastest players I've ever seen, a majestic runner and I think that his nickname in Pakistan was 'like the wind'. Khan used to be able carry the ball on his stick as though it was glued to it, and in a straight line effortlessly beat all his opponents. He had a show-business streak in him and would play with his markers, sometimes standing stock still, then pushing the ball past them and waving them to run and collect it! They never managed it and of course the crowds loved it! I remember him leading Dave Whitaker a real dance during one match, and in the end Dave became a right-half that was positioned just outside the circle! He simply couldn't keep up with the pace of Khan and had no answer to his tantalizing skills.

Hanif Khan, a former Pakistan captain who played inside-left was another of their all-time greats. Again he had all the wonderful skills and could pass the ball with unbelievable deception. He would look one way and give an inch-perfect pass the other. Another of his qualities was his mobility and he could not only bend and swerve but he could stop suddenly at full speed to lose a marker and instantly change direction. One of our trainers once did a survey on Pakistani players and discovered that Hanif Khan ran five miles during the course of a game – far in excess of any other player. What also materialised was that Hanif only ever trained with a stick and a ball. He would go on testing training runs in Karachi with a stick and ball and run up and down banks, round lamp posts and amongst houses. Of course, in hockey that is what will differentiate between someone who can run 100 metres in 11 seconds and a fast hockey player. It's the ability to run at speed in complete control of the ball, and stop and start, that makes a great hockey player.

Aktar Razool was a centre-half who played for Pakistan, whose nickname was 'the camel'. He got the name because he appeared so lumbering and yet during the time that Pakistan were at their best he was the master at tackling and distributing. He had a well-known rivalry with the Australian centre-half, Trevor Smith, and they were always trying to outplay one another. Inevitably it was a fascinating match within a match! They would always resort to a slanging-match abusing one another where they could and attempting to foil each other with their skills. I remember Aktar once saying on Pakistan television that Pakistan was a far superior side to Australia and always would be as long as Australia persisted with such a poor centre-half, and that Trevor Smith had no skills or finesse!

Islah-Uddin was a good Pakistani friend of mine who I first met in 1978. That was towards the end of his playing career when he was captain and it was also the during days when Paul Litjens was scoring with most of his penalty corner shots. I watched the final between Pakistan and Holland and noticed Islah-Uddin break the line, run out and charge down five in every six corners. He would be lined up and no matter what they tried he foiled their attempts. It was incredible and demonstrated the fierce determination of the man. He had immaculate manners, very Westernised in a lot of his ways but a great believer in Pakistani hockey. Sadly, a team he was in charge of was once caught smuggling in some television sets from a trip and as a result Islah-Uddin was dropped from his managerial position in the team. I feel, however, that he should still be accorded respect for all he has achieved and for his belief that the game must come first.

I couldn't talk about great players without mentioning Richard Charlesworth, the Australian inside-forward. A multi-talented man, he has captained Australia, is a medical doctor, an MP, and former Western Australian cricketer. I must admit that I never really got to know 'Charlie' off the pitch, but I do know that he was a formidable competitor on it and we had great mutual respect for another. I have spoken about the incident at the Seoul Olympics when he wouldn't shake my hand after we had beaten Australia in the semi-final, and we have never spoken since. I was speaking at a function in Australia at which he was present and I referred to him as a perfectly balanced Australian – a chip on both shoulders!

The opposite to Rick is Terry Walsh, an Australian centre-forward with rickety knees who was the most recent Sean Kerly of hockey. He didn't have finesse but he sure could find the back of the net! Terry was a marvellous competitor and he's bundled me and the ball into the back of the goal to score on several occasions! He always apologised afterwards and felt it was all part of the game, although he would never want to hurt you. Of the many, many Australians I've met I think Terry was their greatest hockey ambassador. A competitive sportsman on the pitch, he was a gentleman and character off it.

There are also numerous players that I've come across and played with, for and against, who deserve a mention. Neil Mallett who plays for Bournville sticks in my memory because when he was first selected for England he was asked what impressed him most he replied: 'I like the free pair of trainers we get!'.

The others I've picked out have made notable incisions in my memory for either being, doing or participating in something particular. I'll begin with Suti Khehar, a Kenyan Asian of British nationality, who played with distinction for England and Great Britain on over 80 occasions. He had the immense courage to take up a coaching position in South Africa and in spite of all the derisive comments he had to put up with, he went nonetheless. I know he was a hero in South Africa for what he did and he proved to be incredibly popular and successful. I admire him for having the guts to stand up for what he believed in and for going there to see for himself what the situation was and doing what he could to help. It was a brave social act and I want to give him credit for it.

I'd like to mention Andy Churcher next who was a club player for Slough and who never gave less than 100%. Sadly he died of leukemia in 1988. My greatest disappointment was that he was a player who was proud to play for his club, gave all but on his death was suffering financially. If all the people who had played against Andy dug into their pockets and gave just £1 I feel sure it would help the family enormously. His finest performance must have been in 1980 when Slough won the European Championships. It was a tough tournament, and one of the Dutch clubs had 11 internationals in their side. Andy gave so much to the team in that tournament, and I feel that it is a lasting and fitting tribute to his loyally that he scored Slough's winning goal at a corner.

Every sport has its enigma and in hockey it must be Mike Corby. He was immensely talented – I think he was an international squash player, could have been an international tennis player, and won 98 caps for England and Great Britain at indoor and outdoor hockey. However, despite his wonderful talents, and everyone telling him so, he was totally undisciplined, didn't train and was a complete disappointment on the pitch. He just didn't show the commitment necessary to make the most of his undeniable natural ability.

The club character who has impressed me most has simply got to be 'The Duck' or David Payne from East Grinstead. He used to be my stand-in as a goalkeeper, a tremendously cheerful bloke who never complained and who was I think a very under-rated player. He's called the duck because his feet play out at a 45-degree angle and when he gets excited he garbles on and almost sounds like a quacking duck! David is a perpetual prankster and can never be serious, always telling a joke and getting up to no good! But what I also love about him is his contribution to junior hockey. Long before the game of mini hockey was introduced he was setting up tournaments, trips to Europe and helping the less fortunate. There is no selfish side to him at all and I remember him lending me his car once, without a moment's hesitation, when mine had broken down at the club and I had to go out with Julie to an evening function. He also encouraged my son, Simon, aged 14 months, to play hockey. A lovely story concerns a lad who only had one arm. David got him along to the club and spent many patient hours with him, with the result that at the end of the season the lad won the award for gaining maximum points on the merit award scheme.

I wish there were hundreds of Stefan Bloechers in every club in every country because the man is great for the game. The West German centre forward is arrogant but trains hard, he is very expensive but he has talent, drive and should be watched at every possible opportunity. I will never tire of watching him and I think he's one of the idols in the game. Stefan only wears expensive designer clothes, the right after-shave and so on and I suppose could be said to be a bit of a poser! Even so he has kept himself on top of the pedestal by maintaining certain standards. We once played together in a World XI game in Karachi for Islah-Uddin's benefit in front of about 76,000 spectators and the television cameras. As happens in these matches we didn't keep to our formation and it wasn't surprising to see the full-back up at centre-forward and strikers in the defence! On this occasion Stefan was playing full-back and a shot came in which I saved. The ball rolled to Stefan who, with the Pakistani forwards bearing down on him, coolly passed it to me. With the Pakistanis changing direction for me I dummied them and side-footed the ball back to Stefan and we kept this up for a while. Inevitably we were robbed and with the Pakistanis about to shoot, both Stefan and I charged back to the goalmouth to try and save the shot. We were in a hopeless situation and as we dived to block the shot we both ended up in a crumpled heap much to the amusement of the huge crowd!

Neil Hawgood, left-wing for Australia, is one of the new breed of players. I think he's a smashing bloke, very cheerful and a shining example of how to be unorthodox. There are no textbook situations for him and he's a master of adapting his play to all sorts circumstances. I've seen him reverse chip a ball (and put it past my ear into the net!) and even scoop up the ball tennis fashion on the reverse and volley it with one hand. In our semi-final match against Australia in Seoul we had a tremendous battle with the Aussies. The scores were level at 2–2 and a ball came across from their wing and I dived headlong to intercept as did Hawgood and we crashed into one another. We hit heads, and because I had a helmet on and he didn't he came off far worse. As we helped one another up off the ground he said: 'It's not going to be my day. Not only do we look like losing but I've got a bloody great headache as well!'.

Another German, Carsten Fischer, always has the beer and cigarettes in his room after matches! Carsten also thoroughly enjoys playing, and an incident with Ties Kruize in an exhibition match amply demonstrates this. Ties had developed the technique of bouncing the ball on his stick and then volleying the ball, cricket style, up the length of the pitch. Just before there was a rule change banning it, Ties illustrated this technique by knocking the ball up field. It dropped to Carsten who returned the ball in the same way! This game of tennis went on for a while with the crowd captivated by their skill, and it became quite a competition. Eventually Carsten hit the ball on the full and it took off and disappeared out of the stadium! I have never seen anyone hit a ball so far before or since. Just as he hit it and it vanished from sight, Carsten turned to the crowd and said: 'I think the ball was cracked!'

I was involved in another exhibition game with Carsten, following close on the heels of an international we had played against each other. He was trying to establish himself as the hardest hitter in the game, and I was again attempting to prove myself to be the best goalkeeper. We went out to warm up, and I thought I'd take it easy. Carsten started off very gently and then asked if I wanted a few shots. It wasn't exactly as I had anticipated and he let fly with a scorcher that hit me painfully on my knee. The battle commenced! We entertained the crowd for some time and finally he came with a powerful drive that he thought would give me no chance. It went to my top left corner, and I flung myself into the air to save it. There was a huge cheer as I saved it followed by a roar of laughter! What had happened was that the ball had gone up my glove, and as I was diving the force of the ball had removed the glove. Both glove and ball ended up in the net!

Our Great Britain squad have had many laughs at Steve Batchelor's expense because of the way he follows Sean Kerly. He has loads of talent and although he failed on the European professional tennis circuit I hope that the Olympic success will help give him the psychological strength that is required to succeed. But he is a most amusing character in his own right and a popular member of the squad.

I can't mention Great Britain without talking about Sean Kerly, who is one of the greatest goalscorers in hockey today.

Our game was always centred on the theory that if we got the ball to Sean in the circle he would put it in the net. His most outstanding characteristic is his determination – he will simply do anything to try and score. I think the common quote about him is that he is one of the world's great unqualified coaches! Sean loves to talk about the game and tell people what to do, and the controversial incident when he publicly castigated Roger Self during the Olympic match against South Korea showed this well. It was the first match of the tournament, and Self unwisely made two substitutions when we were leading 2–0. We subsequently drew 2–2, and Kerly's outburst was lapped up by the tabloids! British hockey collected more headlines that day than at any other time in history!

Sean is Britain's first hockey superstar, and it will be interesting to see how he handles the attentions of the media and how his career will develop. He may be aggressive and arrogant, but he is also a winner and that sets him apart from everyone else. He was sent off in a match shortly after coming back from Seoul and that received unprecedented media coverage, but he was quick to apologise for his actions. I believe that if Sean Kerly if perceived as being hockey's 'bad boy', then there's not a lot wrong with the sport. I remember what an unrefined player he was when he first came to the team but he has worked hard and realised that he isn't as magnificent as he thought he was. There is no doubt that he has played a key role in all Britain's successes, and British hockey wouldn't be where it is today without him.

The British right-half Jon Potter has the nickname 'ice man' for obvious reasons. A well-liked chap off the field, he is in my opinion one of the best right-halves in the world. His coolness on the pitch has rescued the team on many occasions, and he is a master of turning defence in to attack. Jon has an incredible ability to maintain his concentration and cool throughout a game, and this quality combined with his natural talent, sets him apart from most other defenders.

Going back quite a long time I remember a chap called Peter Freitag, who became assistant coach to the Australian women's gold medal team in Seoul. Before he went to Australia he played full-back for England and Great Britain, and one year we were preparing for the World Cup by practising penalty corners for the benefit of sports correspondent Ian Wooldridge who wanted an in-depth look at hockey. Roger Self was goading the striker Steve Long, telling him he couldn't score and making him hit the ball harder and harder. The ball was being pushed out slower and slower with the result that Steve was coming into the circle closer and closer to the goal. It began to get a bit frightening and eventually Steve was smashing the ball in from close to the penalty spot! I wasn't terribly well protected in those days and was dressed in shorts and a t-shirt as I stood next to Peter who was guarding one of the posts. The next shot from Steve was like a rocket and went straight for Peter's forehead. I dived in front of him and tipped it round the corner. Peter didn't move and when Roger asked him why he hadn't moved, he replied with an ashen face: 'Because I've just shit myself!' Ian loved the story he had witnessed and we all realised how close Peter had come to being badly hurt.

I'm sure Roger Self merits a book about him on his own. In my opinion, when he started in management he simply had no idea. He knew almost nothing about hockey and tactics when he began but he was astute enough to learn. His personnel management was diabolical, however. He would aggravate players and try to get them to react in order to motivate them and I think he ruined several players. It was the only way he knew how to get a response from people.

His great strength, and what hockey has to be thankful for, was his determination to make his political and ideological beliefs known and stick by them. Roger wasn't afraid to say what he thought and, if necessary, he would take action to get it done. He has made valuable contributions to selection and playing performances but his single most valuable contribution was to get Britain to the Olympic Games and help them to succeed. He got us to the Games in the right physical condition and in the right frame of mind and without him Great Britain could never have won the gold medal.

Roger is a character who attracts attention and he now seems to accept all the jibes about the size of his nose and nicknames like 'the beak' and 'jaws'! One great story about him was when we playing in a tournament in Malaysia and the day after a match we were watching a video of the game. He was analysing why a goal had been scored, berating certain people for poor marking and was pointing out various players in the opposing side who were unmarked and asking why. He jabbed his finger at one player and banged it up and down the screen saying: 'And who's that player there and what's he doing roaming free? Look at him in all that space!'

And amidst loud guffaws from the team one of the players said: 'But Roger, he's the umpire!'

10
My World XI

In choosing my World XI, I have selected players that have played with or against me during my international career. I don't think that some of those I've chosen are the best in certain positions, but my criteria was the player in a particular position with the best attitude to the game in terms of sport and sporting behaviour. All of the players were chosen on their best form at the height of their careers.

As it's my team I have selected myself as goalkeeper. It's also because this is the team that I would love to be able to take on tours and play exhibition matches with all round the world, in order to demonstrate what a fantastic game hockey is. I must emphasise that I would play in the same reckless and entertaining style of Carrera, the Spanish goalkeeper!

The reason I have chosen Klaus Kleiter is because I consider him to be the best coach there is and I know he has the ability to get the best out of a team, even though he may not necessarily have the best players. He's flexible in his thinking, has wonderful vision within the game and is always prepared to investigate new possibilities.

WORLD XI

Ian C.B. Taylor (England)
Michael Peter (West Germany)
Paul Litjens (Holland)
Ekkhard Schmidt-Opper (West Germany)
Ties Kruize (Holland)
Ajit Pal Singh (India)
Richard Charlesworth (Australia)
Hanif Khan (Pakistan)
Islah-Uddin (Pakistan)
Stefan Bloecher (West Germany)
Samiullah Khan (Pakistan)

Coach: Klaus Kleiter (West Germany)

INDEX